Knorr®

Fast & Flavorful

Fast & Flavorful

Each recipe in the *Knorr®* *Fast & Flavorful* cookbook was developed in the Knorr Creative Kitchens by professional home economists, then retested by members of our consumer panel to assure easy, delicious results.

The preparation time given with each recipe is the approximate time required to assemble that recipe before cooking, baking or chilling. This includes the time needed for chopping or browning ingredients. A cook, bake or broil time also is indicated. For these times, minimal attention only, such as occasional stirring or checking for doneness, is required.

This symbol denotes that these recipes can be ready to serve in less than 30 minutes.

On the cover: **ORANGE-PEPPERCORN CHICKEN** *(recipe, page 53)*

CONTENTS

From informal creamy dips to elegant savory soups, you can rely on KNORR products to add the right touch.

Spring Vegetable Quiche
(*recipe, page 14*)

Pasta, rice and vegetables are simple to make and ever-so delicious—courtesy of KNORR soup, sauce and rice mixes.

Rice Pilaf El Greco
(*recipe, page 28*)

Get a jump start on easy entrées with KNORR sauce and rice mixes. This collection of delectable dishes was inspired by some of the world's finest chefs.

Pizza Rosa
(*recipe, page 48*)

Mealtime preparation goes on "fast forward" with these speedy recipes made with timesaving KNORR products.

Calypso Pork Roast
(*recipe, page 82*)

The Story of the *Knorr* Brand

KNORR is a name that has stood for high quality for more than 150 years. Recognized by fine cooks around the globe, KNORR food products are unique for both their flavor and convenience.

Carl Heinrich Knorr, a produce wholesaler in Germany, is credited with founding the world-renowned brand in 1838. However, his two sons, young Carl and Alfred, were instrumental in shaping the products as we know them today. The brothers were educated in France, and it was there that they first sampled powders that magically turned into delectable soups when simmered with water.

Today, there are more than 100 convenient, flavor-packed KNORR products in the United States. Talented chefs whose culinary skills span the globe create KNORR products that are enjoyed from coast to coast. Included are savory soups, sauces, gravies, dips, seasoned rices, meal makers and more.

The KNORR *Fast & Flavorful* cookbook is designed for busy families who enjoy great-tasting food. Chock-full of ideas and recipes, it shows you how KNORR products speed meal preparation with sensational results.

Knorr®*...where taste is everything!*®

Appetizers & Starters

Appetizers and starters make any meal special. For your next get-together, try one of our many simple-to-fix dips or soups. Or, prepare sensational-looking, yet easy-to-make, party food. With KNORR, your meal will feel like a celebration.

SPINACH DIP (RECIPE, PAGE 8)

Spinach Dip

MAKES
ABOUT
4 CUPS

PREP TIME:
10 MINUTES

CHILL TIME:
2 HOURS

What could be easier or tastier than this KNORR classic? Just mix, chill and serve with your favorite dippers (photo, pages 6-7).

1 package (10 oz) frozen chopped spinach, thawed and drained
1 container (16 oz) sour cream
1 cup *Hellmann's* or *Best Foods* mayonnaise
1 package (1.4 oz) KNORR Vegetable Soup and Recipe Mix

1 can (8 oz) water chestnuts, drained and chopped (optional)
3 green onions, chopped
Devonsheer or *Old London* melba rounds
JJ Flats flavorall breadflats
Cut-up vegetables

❶ In medium bowl stir spinach, sour cream, mayonnaise, soup mix, water chestnuts and green onions until well mixed.
❷ Cover; chill 2 hours to blend flavors.
❸ Stir before serving. If desired, spoon into *round bread bowl* and garnish with *carrot tops* or *celery leaves.* Serve with melba rounds, breadflats or vegetables as dippers.

Yogurt-Spinach Dip: In step 1, substitute 1 container (16 oz) *plain lowfat yogurt* for sour cream. Makes about 4 cups.

Spinach and Cheese Dip: In step 1, add 2 cups (8 oz) shredded *Swiss cheese* with spinach. Makes 5 cups.

Hot Artichoke Dip

MAKES
ABOUT
2½ CUPS

PREP TIME:
10 MINUTES

BAKE TIME:
25 TO 30
MINUTES

Whether you're having a formal or informal gathering, this time-honored favorite is a winner every time.

1 can (14 oz) artichoke hearts, drained and chopped
¾ cup sour cream
¾ cup *Hellmann's* or *Best Foods* mayonnaise

1 package (0.8 oz) KNORR Onion Chive Dip Mix
⅛ to ¼ teaspoon hot pepper sauce
Devonsheer or *Old London* melba rounds

❶ In small bowl combine artichokes, sour cream, mayonnaise, dip mix and hot pepper sauce. Spoon into small ovenproof dish.
❷ Bake in 350°F oven 25 to 30 minutes or until bubbly.
❸ Serve with melba rounds.

Even Faster Dips

Dips are always a favorite snack or party food—and it's no wonder! They're flavorful and as easy as 1–2–3. Try these new twists on some favorite KNORR dips.

KNORR Cracked Pepper Ranch Dip Mix

Peppery Blue Cheese Dip (photo, page 11)

Stir 1 package *KNORR Cracked Pepper Ranch Dip Mix*, 1 cup *Hellmann's* or *Best Foods* mayonnaise and ¼ cup *sour cream* until smooth.

Stir in: ¼ cup (2 oz) crumbled *blue cheese* plus ¼ to ⅓ cup *milk* until desired consistency.

Rosy Pepper Ranch Dip

Stir 1 package *KNORR Cracked Pepper Ranch Dip Mix* and 1 container (16 oz) *sour cream* until smooth.

Stir in: 1 large *tomato*, seeded and chopped, plus ½ cup *Hellmann's* or *Best Foods* mayonnaise.

KNORR Chili Caliente Dip Mix

Caliente Avocado Dip

Stir 1 package *KNORR Chili Caliente Dip Mix* and 1 container (16 oz) *sour cream* until smooth.

Stir in: 1 medium *avocado*, peeled and chopped, plus ½ cup *Hellmann's* or *Best Foods* mayonnaise.

KNORR Nacho Cheese Dip Mix

Red Pepper Nacho Dip

Stir 1 package *KNORR Nacho Cheese Dip Mix* and 1 container (16 oz) *sour cream* until smooth.

Stir in: 1 jar (7 oz) *roasted red peppers*, drained and chopped.

KNORR Onion Chive Dip Mix

Grand Clam Dip

Stir 1 package *KNORR Onion Chive Dip Mix* and 1 container (16 oz) *sour cream* until smooth.

Stir in: 1 can (6½ oz) *minced clams*, drained.

KNORR Garden Dill Dip Mix

Cucumber-Dill Dip

Stir 1 package *KNORR Garden Dill Dip Mix* and 1 container (16 oz) *sour cream* until smooth.

Stir in: 1 medium *cucumber*, peeled, seeded and chopped, and ½ cup *Hellmann's* or *Best Foods* mayonnaise.

See page 14 for classic dips made with KNORR soup mixes.

Peppery Chicken Nuggets

**MAKES
10 SERVINGS**

**PREP TIME:
5 MINUTES**

**BAKE TIME:
15 MINUTES**

Tender chunks of chicken take on a new personality in this spicy appetizer.

$1\frac{1}{2}$ pounds boneless, skinless chicken
    breasts, cut into 1-inch cubes
2 tablespoons *Mazola* corn oil
$\frac{1}{2}$ cup *Devonsheer* or *Old London*
    plain bread crumbs

1 package (1.1 oz) KNORR Cracked
    Pepper Ranch Dip Mix
Mazola No Stick corn oil
    cooking spray
Peppery Blue Cheese Dip
    (recipe, page 9)

❶ In medium bowl toss chicken with corn oil until coated.
❷ In large plastic food bag combine bread crumbs and dip mix. Add chicken pieces, half at a time; shake to coat. Place on cookie sheet sprayed with cooking spray.
❸ Bake in 375°F oven 15 minutes or until tender.
❹ Serve with blue cheese dip.

Baked Nacho Potatoes

**MAKES
6 SERVINGS**

**PREP TIME:
5 MINUTES**

**BAKE TIME:
20 TO 25
MINUTES**

Whether you need a hot snack or tantalizing side dish, these zesty potatoes fit the bill.

3 medium baking potatoes, cut
    lengthwise into wedges
3 tablespoons *Mazola* corn oil
1 package (1 oz) KNORR Nacho
    Cheese Dip Mix

Mazola No Stick corn oil
    cooking spray
Sour cream (optional)

❶ In large plastic food bag toss potato wedges with corn oil until coated. Add dip mix; shake until potatoes are coated. Place on cookie sheet sprayed with cooking spray.
❷ Bake in 400°F oven 20 to 25 minutes or until tender.
❸ If desired, serve with sour cream.

CLOCKWISE FROM TOP LEFT: BAKED NACHO POTATOES,
PEPPERY BLUE CHEESE DIP (RECIPE, PAGE 9),
PEPPERY CHICKEN NUGGETS

Savory Cheesecake

MAKES
ABOUT
20 SERVINGS

PREP TIME:
12 MINUTES

BAKE TIME:
50 MINUTES

Your guests will never know how effortless it was to make this impressive dish. Serve it as a first course or as a party hors d'oeuvre.

Mazola No Stick corn oil
  cooking spray
3 tablespoons *Devonsheer* or
  Old London plain bread crumbs
12 ounces cream cheese, softened
2 eggs
1 package (1.3 oz) KNORR Parma Rosa
  Pasta Sauce Mix
1 jar (7 oz) roasted red peppers, drained
  and finely chopped

3 green onions, chopped (about ½ cup)
½ cup (2 oz) shredded Jarlsberg or
  Gouda cheese
¼ cup milk
Devonsheer or *Old London* melba
  rounds or thinly sliced French
  bread

❶ Spray bottom of 8-inch springform pan with the cooking spray; sprinkle with the bread crumbs.

❷ In large mixing bowl beat cream cheese and eggs with mixer on medium speed about 5 minutes or until smooth. Blend in sauce mix, roasted red peppers, green onions, cheese and milk. Pour into prepared pan.

❸ Bake in 350°F oven 50 minutes or until knife inserted halfway between center and edge comes out clean. Cool completely in pan.

❹ Remove cheesecake from pan. If desired, press chopped *fresh parsley* around side to garnish. Serve with melba rounds or bread.

Bean Dip

MAKES
ABOUT
1¾ CUPS

PREP TIME:
10 MINUTES

CHILL TIME:
1 HOUR

Cumin gives this dip its Mediterranean flair.

1 can (19 oz) cannellini beans, rinsed
  and drained
1 package (1.4 oz) KNORR French
  Onion Soup and Recipe Mix
¼ cup boiling water
¾ teaspoon ground cumin

⅓ cup *Hellmann's* or *Best Foods*
  mayonnaise
⅓ cup sour cream
2 tablespoons chopped fresh parsley
  Cut-up vegetables

❶ In blender or food processor container combine beans, soup mix, boiling water and cumin. Cover; blend or process 1 minute or until smooth, scraping sides of container once.

❷ Add mayonnaise, sour cream and parsley. Blend or process until combined. Cover; chill to blend the flavors.

❸ Serve with vegetables as dippers.

SAVORY CHEESECAKE

Spring Vegetable Quiche

**MAKES
4 TO 6**
SERVINGS

**PREP TIME:
10** MINUTES

**BAKE TIME:
50** MINUTES

Thanks to the convenience of KNORR soup mix, this quiche makes a quick, satisfying lunch or light supper.

  4 eggs
1½ cups milk
  1 cup (4 oz) shredded Swiss cheese
  1 package (10 oz) frozen
       chopped spinach, thawed and
       squeezed dry

1 package (0.9 oz) KNORR Spring
     Vegetable Soup and Recipe Mix
1 (9-inch) unbaked, frozen, deep-dish
     piecrust

❶ Preheat oven and cookie sheet to 350°F.
❷ In large bowl lightly beat eggs with wire whisk. Blend in milk, cheese, spinach and soup mix. Pour into frozen piecrust.
❸ Bake on cookie sheet 50 minutes or until knife inserted halfway between center and edge comes out clean.

Even Faster Dips from KNORR Soup Mixes

These time-honored favorites are easy to prepare with KNORR soup mixes. Serve with cut-up vegetables and Devonsheer or Old London melba rounds.

❶ In medium bowl combine 1 container (16 oz) *sour cream* and ½ cup *Hellmann's* or *Best Foods* mayonnaise; stir in your preferred *KNORR* soup mix (see below).
❷ Cover; chill 2 hours. Stir before serving. Makes about 2½ cups.

French Onion Dip
    Use 1 package (1.4 oz) *KNORR French Onion Soup and Recipe Mix.*

Tomato-Pepper Dip
    Use 1 package (2.4 oz) *KNORR Tomato with Basil Soup and Recipe Mix.*

Vegetable Dip
    Use 1 package (1.4 oz) *KNORR Vegetable Soup and Recipe Mix* or
    1 package (0.9 oz) *KNORR Spring Vegetable Soup and Recipe Mix.*

Leek Dip
    Use 1 package (1.8 oz) *KNORR Leek Soup and Recipe Mix.*

See page 9 for more flavorful KNORR dips.

Spring Vegetable Quiche

Seven-Layer Dip

MAKES
ABOUT
20 SERVINGS

PREP TIME:
25 MINUTES

CHILL TIME:
1 HOUR

Here's a crowd-size dish that's perfect for just about any occasion. Take it to a picnic or a friend's house—everyone will love it!

1 container (16 oz) sour cream
½ cup *Hellmann's* or *Best Foods* mayonnaise
1 package (1 oz) KNORR Chili Caliente Dip Mix
2 ripe medium avocados, peeled and pitted
1 tablespoon lemon juice
½ teaspoon salt

⅛ teaspoon pepper
1 can (16 oz) refried beans
1 medium tomato, seeded and diced
½ cup sliced pitted ripe olives
1 cup (4 oz) shredded cheddar cheese
2 green onions, sliced
Tortilla chips or *Devonsheer* or *Old London* melba rounds

❶ In medium bowl stir sour cream, mayonnaise and dip mix.
❷ In small bowl use fork to mash the avocados with the lemon juice, salt and pepper until smooth.
❸ On large platter spread refried beans about ½ inch thick. Top with avocado mixture, then spread with chili caliente dip mixture. Sprinkle with tomato, olives, cheese and green onions. Cover; chill.
❹ Serve with tortilla chips or melba rounds.

Black Bean Soup

MAKES
6 SERVINGS

PREP TIME:
15 MINUTES

COOK TIME:
20 MINUTES

This soup usually takes hours to prepare. Our version is just as tasty but takes only 35 minutes to make.

1 tablespoon *Mazola* corn oil
2 ribs celery, chopped
1 cup chopped cooked ham
2 cloves garlic, minced
2 cans (19 oz each) black beans, undrained
2 cups water

1 KNORR Chicken or Beef Bouillon Cube
½ teaspoon ground cumin
½ teaspoon pepper
1 bay leaf

❶ In 3-quart saucepan heat corn oil over medium-high heat. Add celery, ham and garlic; stirring constantly, cook 4 minutes.
❷ Add undrained black beans, water, bouillon cube, cumin, pepper and bay leaf. Bring to boil, stirring to dissolve bouillon. Reduce heat, partially cover and simmer 20 minutes.
❸ Remove and discard bay leaf. Remove 1 cup beans with slotted spoon; set aside.
❹ Transfer remaining soup mixture to blender or food processor container, filling it no more than ⅓ full at a time. Cover; blend until smooth. Add reserved beans to soup.

Spinach and Wild Rice Soup

MAKES
4 SERVINGS

Known for its luxurious, nutty flavor, wild rice is really a long-grain marsh grass. Its unique texture adds a special surprise to this creamy soup.

PREP TIME:
10 MINUTES

COOK TIME:
30 MINUTES

1 tablespoon *Mazola* corn oil	2 cups milk
½ cup chopped onion	1 package (1.8 oz) KNORR Cream of
1½ cups water	Spinach Soup and Recipe Mix
¼ cup wild rice	

❶ In 2-quart saucepan heat corn oil over medium-high heat. Add the onion; stirring constantly, cook 4 minutes.

❷ Stir in water and rice; bring to boil. Reduce heat, cover and simmer 15 minutes.

❸ Add the milk and soup mix. Stirring constantly, bring to boil. Reduce the heat, cover and simmer 15 minutes.

Quick Gazpacho

MAKES
4 SERVINGS

For a refreshing summertime meal, serve this cold soup along with cheese and crusty bread.

PREP TIME:
8 MINUTES

CHILL TIME:
1 HOUR

1½ cups water	2 dashes hot pepper sauce or to taste
1 package (1.4 oz) KNORR Vegetable Soup and Recipe Mix	1 small cucumber, peeled, seeded and chopped
1 can (28 oz) whole tomatoes in juice, undrained	1 small green pepper, chopped
½ teaspoon dried basil or 1 teaspoon chopped fresh basil	2 teaspoons cider vinegar
	Brownberry toasted croutons (optional)

❶ In 1-quart saucepan bring water to boil over medium-high heat. Add soup mix; stirring frequently, cook 2 minutes.

❷ Transfer half of the soup to blender or food processor container. Add half of the undrained tomatoes, basil and hot pepper sauce. Cover; blend or process on high speed 1 to 2 minutes or until smooth. Pour into bowl. Repeat with remaining soup and tomatoes.

❸ Stir in cucumber and green pepper. Cover; chill.

❹ Stir in vinegar before serving. If desired, serve with croutons.

Manhattan Clam Chowder

**MAKES
4 TO 6
SERVINGS**

**PREP TIME:
5 MINUTES**

**COOK TIME:
10 MINUTES**

Nothing "fishy" about this quick-fix approach to a restaurant favorite. Just add clams and heat. Don't boil the clams; it toughens them.

1 can (14½ to 16 oz) whole tomatoes in juice, undrained
2 cups water
1 package (1.4 oz) KNORR Vegetable Soup and Recipe Mix

¼ teaspoon dried thyme (optional)
1 can (6.5 oz) minced clams, undrained

❶ In 2-quart saucepan combine undrained tomatoes, water, soup mix and, if desired, thyme. Stir to crush tomatoes.
❷ Bring mixture to boil over medium-high heat. Reduce the heat, partially cover and simmer 10 minutes.
❸ Add the undrained clams. Heat through (do not boil). If desired, garnish with *fresh thyme sprigs.*

Italian Sausage Soup: Prepare Manhattan Clam Chowder as above but omit clams. In step 3, add 1 can (10 oz) *kidney beans*, drained, and ½ pound *Italian sausage*, cooked and sliced. Heat through.

French Onion Soup

**MAKES
3 SERVINGS**

**PREP TIME:
8 MINUTES**

**BROIL TIME:
1 TO 2
MINUTES**

Savor the deep, rich flavors of Provence in this classic soup.

1 package (1.4 oz) KNORR French Onion Soup and Recipe Mix
3 slices French bread
2 tablespoons butter or margarine

½ cup grated Parmesan cheese
½ cup (2 oz) shredded Gruyère or Swiss cheese

❶ Prepare soup mix according to package directions.
❷ Toast bread; spread both sides of bread with butter. In small bowl mix Parmesan and Gruyère cheeses.
❸ Ladle soup into 3 ovenproof bowls; place in shallow baking pan. Top with toast; sprinkle with cheese mixture.
❹ Broil 1 to 2 minutes or until cheese is bubbly and lightly browned.

LEFT TO RIGHT:
MANHATTAN CLAM CHOWDER,
FRENCH ONION SOUP

Pesto Bread

MAKES
2 LOAVES

PREP TIME:
5 MINUTES

BAKE TIME:
10 MINUTES

Serve one loaf crusty and hot—freeze the other for a day when you're short on time. These zesty loaves are ideal with pasta or barbecue.

⅓ cup olive oil
1 package (0.5 oz) KNORR Pesto Pasta Sauce Mix

2 loaves Italian bread, halved lengthwise
1 cup (4 oz) shredded mozzarella cheese

❶ In small bowl blend olive oil and sauce mix. Brush on cut surfaces of bread; sprinkle with cheese.
❷ Place four loaf halves* on cookie sheet, cheese-side up.
❸ Bake in 350°F oven 10 minutes or until cheese melts. Slice.

*If desired, wrap two or more loaf halves in foil and freeze. To prepare: Thaw, unwrap and place on cookie sheet. Bake as in step 3.

Escarole Soup

MAKES
9 SERVINGS

PREP TIME:
15 MINUTES

COOK TIME:
20 MINUTES

Escarole has broad, slightly curved leaves ranging in color from dark green to pale yellow. Simmer it briefly in the vegetable-chicken broth to make this garden-fresh-tasting soup.

1 tablespoon *Mazola* corn oil
½ cup chopped onion
1 carrot, peeled and sliced
1 clove garlic, minced
2 quarts water
3 KNORR Chicken Bouillon Cubes or 2 tablespoons KNORR Concentrated Chicken flavor Broth

1 package (5.7 oz) KNORR Mushroom Risotto Rice Mix
1 small head escarole (about 1¼ lb), cut into bite-size pieces
1 cup diced cooked chicken (optional)
Freshly grated Parmesan cheese (optional)
Freshly ground pepper (optional)

❶ In 4-quart Dutch oven heat corn oil over medium-high heat. Add onion, carrot and garlic; stirring frequently, cook 5 minutes or until vegetables are tender.
❷ Add the water and the bouillon. Bring mixture to boil, stirring to dissolve bouillon cubes. Stir in the rice mix. Reduce heat, cover and simmer 15 minutes or until rice is tender, stirring occasionally.
❸ Add escarole and, if desired, chicken; simmer 5 minutes.
❹ If desired, serve with freshly grated Parmesan cheese and freshly ground pepper.

Even Faster Soups

KNORR soups are delicious just the way they are, but an added touch makes them extra special. To make your next bowl of KNORR soup extraordinary, prepare the soup mix according to package directions, then stir in some of our flavorings (see below).

KNORR French Onion Soup and Recipe Mix

Cheese Deluxe: Stir in 2 to 3 ounces diced *Brie*.
The Quick Classic: Add shredded *Swiss cheese;* top with *Brownberry croutons*.

KNORR Tomato with Basil Soup and Recipe Mix

A Touch of Bacon: Add 2 to 3 slices crumbled cooked *bacon* or use bottled bacon pieces.
Tomato-Chicken Soup: Add diced cooked *chicken*.

KNORR Leek Soup and Recipe Mix

Ham It Up: Add diced cooked *ham*.
Easy Corn Chowder: Add *cream-style corn*.
Creamy: Prepare with *half-and-half* or *light cream*.

KNORR Spring Vegetable Soup and Recipe Mix

Chicken Vegetable: Add diced cooked *chicken*.
Double Vegetables: Stir in diced *zucchini* or *tomato*.

KNORR Vegetable Soup and Recipe Mix

Busy-Day Lunch: Add diced cooked *ham*.
Rice or Pasta: Add cooked *rice* or *noodles*.
Vegetarian: Add 1 can *kidney beans*, rinsed and drained.

KNORR Chicken Flavor Noodle Soupmix

Greek: Stir in 1 to 2 tablespoons *lemon juice*.
Tomato: Add l large *tomato*, seeded and diced.
Chicken-Corn Soup: Add *cream-style corn*.

KNORR Oxtail Soup and Recipe Mix

Gourmet: Add 2 to 3 tablespoons *sherry*.
Russian Borscht: Add diced cooked *beets*.
Noodlin' Around: Add cooked *noodles*.

Vegetables & Side Dishes

Spoon one of these vegetables, salads, rices or pastas onto your plate, and a simple meal becomes much more enticing. Use KNORR soup, sauce and rice mixes to add a chef's touch to your recipes in a moment.

CLOCKWISE FROM TOP LEFT:
ONION-ROASTED POTATOES (RECIPE, PAGE 24),
FRESH VEGETABLE SKILLET (RECIPE, PAGE 24),
LEMON VEGETABLES (RECIPE, PAGE 25)

Fresh Vegetable Skillet

MAKES
6 SERVINGS

Keep this quick-cooking recipe at your fingertips; it can be made with almost any assortment of vegetables that you have on hand (photo, pages 22-23).

TOTAL PREP TIME:
20 MINUTES

2 tablespoons *Mazola* corn oil	⅓ cup water
2 large zucchini, cubed	1 KNORR Vegetarian Vegetable
1 large red pepper, cubed	Bouillon Cube
1 large yellow pepper, cubed	½ teaspoon dried basil
1 medium onion, diced	¼ teaspoon dried oregano
4 cloves garlic, minced	¼ teaspoon pepper

❶ In large skillet heat corn oil over medium-high heat. Add zucchini, red and yellow peppers, onion and garlic; stirring frequently, cook 5 minutes.
❷ Add water, bouillon cube, basil, oregano and pepper. Bring to boil, stirring to dissolve bouillon cube. Reduce heat to low; cover and simmer 5 minutes, stirring occasionally.

Onion-Roasted Potatoes

MAKES
6 TO 8
SERVINGS

For an uncomplicated oven dinner, bake chicken breasts, pork chops, meat loaf or fish in a pan alongside these potatoes (photo, pages 22-23).

PREP TIME:
5 MINUTES

BAKE TIME:
35 MINUTES

2 tablespoons *Mazola* corn oil	½ teaspoon rosemary, crushed (optional)
1 package (1.4 oz) KNORR French	2 pounds medium all-purpose or red
Onion Soup and Recipe Mix	bliss potatoes, quartered

❶ Pour corn oil into 13x9x2-inch baking pan. Add soup mix, rosemary, if desired, and potatoes; toss to coat.
❷ Bake in 375°F oven, stirring occasionally, 35 minutes or until potatoes are tender.

Company-Best Vegetables in a Jiffy

It's easy to make vegetables extra special with KNORR sauce mixes. The most popular choices for vegetables are KNORR Hollandaise, Bearnaise and White Sauce mixes. For even more quick sauce ideas, see pages 90 and 91.

Lemon Vegetables

MAKES 4 SERVINGS

TOTAL PREP TIME: 20 MINUTES

Heavenly KNORR Hollandaise Sauce Mix transforms ordinary vegetables into tantalizing party fare (photo, pages 22-23).

½ cup milk
¼ cup water
1 package (0.9 oz) KNORR Hollandaise Sauce Mix
1 to 2 teaspoons lemon juice
¾ teaspoon ground ginger

2 tablespoons *Mazola* corn oil
½ pound green beans, trimmed
2 cups broccoli florets
1 medium onion, cut into thin wedges
2 carrots, sliced
1 clove garlic, minced

❶ In bowl stir milk, water, sauce mix, lemon juice and ginger until blended; set aside.
❷ In large skillet heat corn oil over medium-high heat. Stirring quickly and frequently, cook green beans, broccoli, onion, carrots and garlic 5 minutes.
❸ Stir sauce mixture; pour into skillet. Stirring constantly, bring to boil; boil 1 minute.

Spinach Formaggio

MAKES 4 SERVINGS

TOTAL PREP TIME: 10 MINUTES

Formaggio is the Italian word for cheese. Not just for pasta, KNORR four-cheese pasta sauce (made with Parmesan, Romano, blue and cream cheeses) turns frozen spinach into a special dish.

1½ cups milk
2 packages (10 oz each) frozen chopped spinach, thawed and well drained

1 package (1.5 oz) KNORR Four Cheese Toscana Pasta Sauce Mix
1 tablespoon butter or margarine

❶ In 2-quart saucepan combine milk, spinach, sauce mix and butter. Stirring constantly, bring to boil over medium-high heat.
❷ Reduce heat to low; stirring occasionally, simmer 6 minutes.

Thai Lemon Rice

MAKES
4 SERVINGS

PREP TIME:
15 MINUTES

COOK TIME:
15 MINUTES

The intriguing essence of Southeast Asian cooking is featured in this no-fuss recipe.

1¾ cups water
 1 tablespoon soy sauce
 ½ teaspoon ground ginger
 ⅛ teaspoon crushed red pepper
 1 package (5.1 oz) KNORR Lemon
        Herb with Jasmine Rice Pilaf
        Rice Mix

 2 cups diced cooked pork or chicken
 2 ounces snow peas
 ¼ cup chopped salted peanuts (optional)
 3 tablespoons chopped fresh cilantro
        (optional)
 4 green onions, sliced (optional)

❶ In large skillet bring water, soy sauce, ginger and crushed red pepper to a boil. Stir in rice mix; return to boil. Reduce heat, cover and simmer 15 minutes.
❷ Stir in pork and snow peas; cook 5 minutes longer or until rice is tender. If desired, sprinkle with peanuts, cilantro and green onions.

Scalloped Potatoes

MAKES
6 SERVINGS

PREP TIME:
15 MINUTES

BAKE TIME:
1 HOUR

Remember Grandma's incredible scalloped potatoes? Here's a streamlined '90s version made with a creamy four-cheese sauce.

  Mazola No Stick corn oil
        cooking spray
 6 medium potatoes, peeled and thinly
        sliced (about 1½ pounds)
 1 medium onion, thinly sliced
 ¼ cup chopped fresh parsley

2½ cups milk
 1 package (1.5 oz) KNORR Four
        Cheese Toscana Pasta Sauce Mix
 ½ teaspoon paprika

❶ Spray 11x7x1½-inch baking dish with cooking spray. In dish layer potatoes, onion and parsley; set aside.
❷ In 2-quart saucepan combine milk, sauce mix and paprika. Stirring constantly, bring to boil over medium heat; boil 1 minute. Pour sauce over potatoes.
❸ Bake in 375°F oven 1 hour or until potatoes are tender.

Scalloped Potatoes and Ham: In step 1, layer 1 cup cubed cooked *ham* over potatoes.

THAI LEMON RICE

Rice Pilaf El Greco

MAKES
4 SERVINGS

PREP TIME:
10 MINUTES

COOK TIME:
20 MINUTES

Traditional pilaf requires browning rice in oil or butter before simmering in a flavorful stock. This Greek-style version starts with KNORR rice mix to speed preparation.

1 tablespoon *Mazola* corn oil
1 small onion, chopped
1¼ cups water
1 package (4.3 oz) KNORR Original Recipe Pilaf Rice Mix

4 cups fresh spinach leaves, rinsed and drained, or ½ of a 10-ounce package frozen leaf spinach, thawed and drained
½ to 1 cup (2 to 4 oz) crumbled feta cheese
1 medium tomato, coarsely chopped

❶ In large skillet heat corn oil over medium-high heat. Add onion; stirring frequently, cook 3 minutes.
❷ Add water; bring to boil. Stir in rice mix; return to boil. Reduce heat, cover and simmer 20 minutes.
❸ Stir in spinach, cheese and chopped tomato. Cover and let stand 3 minutes or until spinach wilts. If desired, garnish with *tomato wedges* and *fresh herbs.*

Black Bean Pilaf

MAKES
6 SERVINGS

PREP TIME:
10 MINUTES

COOK TIME:
15 MINUTES

Here's a lightly seasoned, fiber-rich side dish with the mellow flavor of Spanish rice. Serve with fish, chicken, pork or beef.

1 tablespoon *Mazola* corn oil
2 large cloves garlic, minced
2 cups water
1 can (10 to 15 oz) black beans, rinsed and drained

1 cup frozen corn
1 package (4.7 oz) KNORR Spanish Pilaf Rice Mix

❶ In large skillet heat corn oil over medium-high heat. Add garlic; stirring frequently, cook 1 minute.
❷ Add water, black beans and corn; bring to boil. Stir in rice mix; return to boil. Reduce heat, cover and simmer 15 minutes.
❸ Remove from heat. Let stand 5 minutes.

Rice Pilaf El Greco

Savory Vegetable Pilaf

MAKES
6 SERVINGS

PREP TIME:
7 MINUTES

COOK TIME:
20 MINUTES

The word "pilaf" refers to a rice-based side or main dish. Add cooked chicken, turkey, pork or beef to this side accompaniment and it becomes a light one-dish meal.

1 tablespoon *Mazola* corn oil	1 package (4.3 oz) KNORR Original Recipe Pilaf Rice Mix
2 cloves garlic, minced	
1½ teaspoons ground cumin	1 package (10 oz) frozen mixed vegetables
¼ teaspoon ground cinnamon	
1 cup water	1 large onion, chopped

❶ In 3-quart saucepan heat corn oil over medium-high heat. Add garlic, cumin and cinnamon; stirring frequently, cook 1 minute.

❷ Add water; bring to boil. Stir in rice mix; return to boil. Reduce heat, cover and simmer 10 minutes.

❸ Stir in mixed vegetables and onion. Cover and cook 10 minutes longer or until rice is tender, stirring occasionally.

Primavera Rice Salad

MAKES
6 SERVINGS

PREP TIME:
30 MINUTES

CHILL TIME:
1 HOUR

Looking for interesting ways to include more grains in your diet? Try this delectable rice salad for a change of pace.

1 package (5.6 oz) KNORR Vegetable Primavera Risotto Rice Mix	¼ teaspoon pepper
	1 can (8 oz) corn, drained
2 tablespoons *Mazola* corn oil	1 large tomato, diced
1 tablespoon red wine vinegar	1 small zucchini, diced
1 clove garlic, minced	¼ cup diced red onion
1 teaspoon dried basil	

❶ Prepare rice mix according to package directions; cool.

❷ In large bowl combine corn oil, vinegar, garlic, basil and pepper. Add rice, corn, tomato, zucchini and onion; toss to coat.

❸ Cover; chill to blend flavors.

Even Faster Rice Dishes

KNORR Pilaf Rice Mixes and KNORR Italian Risotto Rice Mixes make taste-tempting, easy-to-prepare side dishes. Stir in beans, fish, poultry or meat for a fast and flavorful meal.

KNORR Italian Risotto Rice or Pilaf Rice Mix (any flavor)

Light Supper
Prepare 1 package (any flavor) *KNORR Italian Risotto Rice Mix* or *KNORR Pilaf Rice Mix* as directed.
Stir in: 8 ounces cut-up cooked *meat, poultry* or *seafood;* heat through.

KNORR Risotto Milanese Rice Mix

Risotto and Peas
Prepare 1 package *KNORR Risotto Milanese Rice Mix* as directed.
Stir in: 1 cup *peas;* heat through.

KNORR Spanish Pilaf Rice Mix

Rice and Bean Pilaf
Prepare 1 package *KNORR Spanish Pilaf Rice Mix* as directed.
Stir in: 1 can (10 to 15 oz) *black beans,* rinsed and drained; heat through.

KNORR Vegetable Primavera Risotto Rice Mix

Italian Risotto
Prepare 1 package *KNORR Vegetable Primavera Risotto Rice Mix* as directed.
Stir in: 1 cup diced cooked *ham;* heat through.

KNORR Original Recipe Pilaf Rice Mix

Nutty Pilaf
Prepare 1 package *KNORR Original Recipe Pilaf Rice Mix* as directed.
Stir in: ½ cup chopped toasted *pecans* or *walnuts* and ¼ cup *dried cranberries* or *cherries.*

KNORR Lemon Herb with Jasmine Rice Pilaf Rice Mix

Oriental Pilaf
Prepare 1 package *KNORR Lemon Herb with Jasmine Rice Pilaf Rice Mix* as directed.
Stir in: ½ cup chopped *peanuts* and 3 *green onions,* sliced.

Red Pepper 'n' Pasta

MAKES 4 TO 6 SERVINGS

TOTAL PREP TIME: 18 MINUTES

The robust flavors of Italy make this fast-to-fix side-dish salad appetizing fare.

3 tablespoons olive oil
1 medium red pepper, finely chopped
1 large clove garlic, minced
½ cup water
1 package (0.5 oz) KNORR Pesto Pasta Sauce Mix

1 teaspoon red wine vinegar
7 ounces *Mueller's* pasta ruffles (about 2½ cups), cooked and drained
Lettuce leaves

❶ In large skillet heat olive oil over medium-high heat. Add red pepper and garlic; stirring frequently, cook 3 minutes.
❷ Blend in water and sauce mix. Stirring occasionally, bring to boil. Reduce heat; simmer 4 minutes. Remove from heat; stir in vinegar.
❸ Pour sauce mixture over pasta and toss to coat. Cool to room temperature.
❹ Spoon pasta onto lettuce-lined plates. If desired, garnish with *yellow pepper strips.*

Pasta 'n' Beans

MAKES 4 SERVINGS

TOTAL PREP TIME: 10 MINUTES

Here's a variation on the Italian classic Pasta E Fagioli. This delightful side dish mingles white beans and twist pasta with a creamy tomato sauce.

1 can (14½ oz) stewed tomatoes, undrained
1 package (1.3 oz) KNORR Parma Rosa Pasta Sauce Mix

1 can (19 oz) cannellini beans, rinsed and drained
8 ounces *Mueller's* twists (about 3 cups), cooked and drained

❶ In 2-quart saucepan combine undrained tomatoes and sauce mix. Stirring and crushing tomatoes with spoon, bring to boil over medium-high heat. Reduce heat; simmer 3 minutes.
❷ Stir in beans; heat through.
❸ Pour over pasta; toss until combined.

RED PEPPER 'N' PASTA

Wilted Spinach 'n' Pasta Salad

**MAKES
6 SERVINGS**

All-time favorite spinach salad gets a hearty twist with the addition of pasta. Serve this dish warm with meat, fish or poultry.

**TOTAL
PREP TIME:
20 MINUTES**

4 ounces fresh spinach, torn into
    bite-size pieces (about 2 cups)
7 ounces *Mueller's* pasta ruffles (about
    2½ cups), cooked, rinsed with cold
    water and drained
4 to 6 slices bacon, chopped (3 to 4 oz)
1 large red or yellow pepper, chopped
    (1 cup)

1 small onion, finely chopped
⅓ cup water
1 KNORR Chicken Bouillon Cube
¼ teaspoon pepper
1 tablespoon cider vinegar

❶ In large bowl combine spinach and pasta; set aside.
❷ In large skillet cook bacon over medium-high heat, stirring frequently until browned. Drain bacon on paper towels. Pour off all but 3 tablespoons drippings. Set bacon aside.
❸ Add red pepper and onion to drippings; stirring frequently, cook 4 minutes. Add water, bouillon cube and pepper. Stirring to dissolve bouillon cube, bring to boil; reduce heat and simmer 2 minutes. Stir in vinegar.
❹ Pour over spinach and pasta. Add bacon and toss to coat. Serve immediately.

Garden Dill Dressing

**MAKES
ABOUT
1½ CUPS**

KNORR sauce and dip mixes can be used to make snappy salad dressings.

1 cup *Hellmann's* or *Best Foods*
    mayonnaise
¾ cup milk

2 tablespoons cider vinegar
1 package (0.7 oz) KNORR Garden
    Dill Dip Mix

**PREP TIME:
5 MINUTES**

**CHILL TIME:
UP TO
1 HOUR**

❶ In small bowl stir mayonnaise, milk, vinegar and dip mix until smooth.
❷ Cover; chill to blend flavors.

Garden Dill-Cucumber Salad

In medium bowl combine 3 *cucumbers*, halved lengthwise and thinly sliced; 1 medium *onion*, thinly sliced; and ½ cup *Garden Dill Dressing*. Toss to coat. Season to taste with *salt* and *pepper*. Chill to blend flavors. Makes 6 to 8 servings.

Pesto Salad Dressing

Makes
About
¾ Cup

Prep Time:
5 minutes

Chill Time:
up to
1 hour

For a quick and delicious pesto salad dressing that doesn't require a blender, use KNORR Pesto Pasta Sauce Mix.

¾ cup olive oil	1 package (0.5 oz) KNORR Pesto Pasta
2 tablespoons red	Sauce Mix
wine vinegar	

❶ In medium bowl and with wire whisk blend olive oil, vinegar and sauce mix.
❷ Cover; chill to blend flavors.

Pesto Tomato Salad *(photo, page 43)*
In large bowl combine 2 cups *cherry tomatoes*, halved; ¼ cup chopped *red onion*; 8 ounces *mozzarella cheese*, cut into ½-inch cubes, and ¼ cup *Pesto Salad Dressing*. Toss to coat. Makes 6 servings.

Onion-Chive Dressing

Makes
About
2 cups

Prep Time:
5 minutes

Chill Time:
up to
1 hour

Wine vinegar adds a tangy, delightful note to this creamy dressing.

1 cup *Hellmann's* or *Best Foods*	2 tablespoons red wine vinegar
mayonnaise	1 package (0.8 oz) KNORR Onion
¾ cup milk	Chive Dip Mix

❶ In medium bowl stir mayonnaise, milk, vinegar and dip mix until well blended.
❷ Cover; chill to blend flavors.

Ham and Vegetable Salad with Onion-Chive Dressing
In large bowl combine 3 cups chopped *iceberg lettuce;* 1 cup diced cooked *ham;* 1 medium *zucchini*, chopped; ½ cup chopped *onion* and ½ cup chopped *red pepper*. Add ½ cup *Onion-Chive Dressing.* Toss to coat. Makes 4 servings.

Create a Quick Flavorful Spread
Pesto Butter: In medium bowl stir 1 cup (2 sticks) *butter* or *margarine*, softened, and 1 package (0.5 oz) *KNORR Pesto Pasta Sauce Mix* until blended.

Spread on corn on the cob or toss with cooked fresh vegetables. Or, spread on French or Italian bread. Wrap bread in foil and bake in 400°F oven or heat on grill 5 to 10 minutes or until butter melts. Makes about 1 cup.

Pasta & Meatless Dishes

Wholesome pastas and effortless vegetarian dishes take center stage in this chapter. KNORR products give you a head start on dinner while pleasantly accenting the foods you serve.

PASTA PRIMAVERA (RECIPE, PAGE 38)

Pasta Primavera

MAKES
4 SERVINGS

TOTAL
PREP TIME:
15 MINUTES

There are an infinite number of ways to make Pasta Primavera—all scrumptious. For this creamy pasta-and-vegetable dish, we suggest using zucchini, mushrooms and red peppers. But, if you like, choose your own selection of fresh or frozen cut-up vegetables (photo, pages 36-37).

2 tablespoons butter or margarine	1⅓ cups milk
1 medium zucchini, halved lengthwise and sliced	1 package (1.5 oz) KNORR Four Cheese Toscana Pasta Sauce Mix
2 cups sliced mushrooms	8 ounces *Mueller's* ridged mostaccioli (about 3 cups), cooked and drained
1 medium red pepper, cut lengthwise into thin strips	Freshly grated Parmesan cheese (optional)
1 small onion, chopped	
2 cloves garlic, minced	

❶ In large skillet heat the butter over medium-high heat. Add zucchini, mushrooms, red pepper, onion and garlic; stirring frequently, cook 5 minutes or until the vegetables are tender-crisp.

❷ Stir in milk and sauce mix. Stirring constantly, bring to boil. Reduce heat; stirring constantly, simmer 1 minute. Remove skillet from heat.

❸ Spoon sauce over pasta. Toss to coat. If desired, sprinkle with Parmesan cheese.

Going Beyond Pasta

When you need a quick sauce for a main-dish casserole or a tasty sauce to serve over cooked vegetables, turn to KNORR pasta sauce mixes. These sauces blend as deliciously with other foods as they do with pasta.

Broccoli Cheese Sauce with Tortellini

MAKES
4 SERVINGS

Here's a 20-minute entrée that will quickly become one of your mealtime standbys.

TOTAL
PREP TIME:
20 MINUTES

1 tablespoon butter or margarine
1 package (10 oz) frozen chopped
    broccoli, thawed and drained
¾ cup water
½ cup milk

1 package (1.5 oz) KNORR Four
    Cheese Toscana Pasta Sauce Mix
1 package (16 oz) frozen meat or
    cheese tortellini, cooked and
    drained

❶ In large skillet heat butter over medium-high heat. Add the broccoli, water, milk and sauce mix. Stirring constantly, bring to boil. Reduce the heat; stirring occasionally, cook 3 minutes.

❷ Spoon over tortellini. Toss to coat.

Shrimp Primavera

MAKES
2 SERVINGS

Dinner for two could hardly be easier or more flavorful.

TOTAL
PREP TIME:
20 MINUTES

2 tablespoons butter or margarine
½ pound shrimp, shelled and deveined
1 clove garlic, minced
1 cup broccoli florets
1 medium red pepper, cut into
    matchstick strips
1 small carrot, cut into matchstick strips
1 cup milk

½ cup water
1 package (1.6 oz) KNORR Alfredo
    Pasta Sauce Mix
8 ounces *Mueller's* thin spaghetti or
    fettuccine, cooked and drained
    Freshly grated Parmesan cheese
    Freshly ground pepper

❶ In medium skillet melt butter over medium-high heat. Add shrimp and garlic; stirring frequently, cook 1 minute. Remove shrimp with slotted spoon.

❷ Add broccoli, red pepper and carrot; stirring frequently, cook 3 minutes. Blend in milk, water and sauce mix. Stirring constantly, bring to boil. Add shrimp. Reduce heat and simmer 2 minutes, stirring occasionally.

❸ Add pasta; toss to coat. Serve immediately with Parmesan cheese and pepper.

Even Faster Sauces for Pasta

Use the magic of KNORR Pasta Sauces for instant, fabulous meals. Try our suggestions below or create your own.

KNORR Alfredo Pasta Sauce Mix

Broccoli-Ham Pasta Sauce
Prepare 1 package *KNORR Alfredo Pasta Sauce Mix* as directed.
Stir in: 2 cups cooked *broccoli florets* and 1 cup diced cooked *ham;* heat. Toss with 8 ounces *cheese tortellini,* cooked.

Sun-Dried Tomato Pasta Sauce
Prepare 1 package *KNORR Alfredo Pasta Sauce Mix* as directed.
Stir in: ¼ cup finely chopped *sun-dried tomatoes* or chopped *roasted red peppers.* Toss with 8 ounces *fettuccine,* cooked.

KNORR Carbonara Pasta Sauce Mix

Creamy Tomato Pasta Sauce
Prepare 1 package *KNORR Carbonara Pasta Sauce Mix* as directed.
Stir in: 1 can (14½ oz) *stewed tomatoes,* drained and chopped. Toss with 8 ounces *mostaccioli* or *penne,* cooked.

Creamy Vegetable Pasta Sauce
Prepare 1 package *KNORR Carbonara Pasta Sauce Mix* as directed.
Stir in: 1 cup cooked cut *green beans* and 1 can (4 oz) *sliced mushrooms,* drained. Toss with 8 ounces *spaghetti,* cooked.

KNORR Four Cheese Toscana Pasta Sauce Mix

Cheesy Chicken Pasta Sauce
Prepare 1 package *KNORR Four Cheese Toscana Pasta Sauce Mix* as directed.
Stir in: 1½ cups chopped cooked *chicken* and ¼ cup sliced, pitted *ripe olives.* Toss with 8 ounces *mostaccioli* or *twist macaroni,* cooked.

Roasted Red Pepper Pasta Sauce
Prepare 1 package *KNORR Four Cheese Toscana Pasta Sauce Mix* as directed.
Stir in: ⅓ cup chopped *roasted red peppers.* Toss with 8 ounces *fettuccine,* cooked.

KNORR Garlic Herb Pasta Sauce Mix

Creamy Peas and Onions Pasta Sauce
Prepare 1 package *KNORR Garlic Herb Pasta Sauce Mix* as directed.
Stir in: 1 package (10 oz) frozen *peas and pearl onions,* thawed and drained. Toss with 8 ounces *cheese* or *meat tortellini,* cooked.

KNORR Garlic Herb Pasta Sauce Mix (continued)

Garlic-Clam Pasta Sauce
Prepare 1 package *KNORR Garlic Herb Pasta Sauce Mix* as directed.
Stir in: 1 can (6½ oz) minced *clams*, drained. Toss with 8 ounces *linguine*, cooked.

Spinach-Bacon Pasta Sauce
Prepare 1 package *KNORR Garlic Herb Pasta Sauce Mix* as directed.
Stir in: 5 ounces (½ of a 10-oz package) frozen chopped *spinach*, thawed and drained,
    and ⅓ cup (about 3 slices) crumbled cooked *bacon*. Toss with 8 ounces *rigatoni*,
    cooked.

KNORR Pesto Pasta Sauce Mix

Chicken-Pesto Pasta Sauce
Prepare 1 package *KNORR Pesto Pasta Sauce Mix* as directed.
Stir in: 1½ cups diced cooked *chicken* and 2 tablespoons chopped *sun-dried tomatoes* or
    roasted red peppers. Toss with 8 ounces *linguine*, cooked.

Tomato-Pignoli Pasta Sauce
Prepare 1 package *KNORR Pesto Pasta Sauce Mix* as directed.
Stir in: 1 cup halved *cherry tomatoes* and ¼ cup chopped toasted *pignoli (pine nuts)* or
    walnuts. Toss with 8 ounces *twist macaroni*, cooked.

KNORR Creamy Pesto Pasta Sauce Mix

Creamy Shrimp-Pesto Pasta Sauce
Prepare 1 package *KNORR Creamy Pesto Pasta Sauce Mix* as directed.
Stir in: 6 ounces cooked medium *shrimp*. Toss with 8 ounces *angel hair pasta* or
    thin spaghetti, cooked.

Ham-Pesto Pasta Sauce
Prepare 1 package *KNORR Creamy Pesto Pasta Sauce Mix* as directed.
Stir in: 1 cup diced cooked *ham*. Toss with 8 ounces *linguine*, cooked.

KNORR Parma Rosa Pasta Sauce Mix

Sausage and Vegetable Pasta Sauce
Prepare 1 package *KNORR Parma Rosa Pasta Sauce Mix* as directed.
Stir in: 6 ounces sliced cooked *sweet Italian sausage* and ½ cup cooked *broccoli florets*.
    Toss with 8 ounces *rigatoni*, cooked.

Creamy Spinach Lasagne

MAKES
6 TO 8
SERVINGS

PREP TIME:
20 MINUTES

BAKE TIME:
30 MINUTES

Spinach teams up with a creamy garlic sauce for a delectable no-meat lasagne that's sure to win rave reviews from your dinner guests.

1 package (1.6 oz) KNORR Garlic Herb Pasta Sauce Mix
1 tablespoon *Mazola* corn oil
1 large onion, chopped
1 clove garlic, minced
1 package (10 oz) frozen chopped spinach, thawed and drained
½ teaspoon dried basil

½ teaspoon salt
¼ teaspoon oregano
1 container (15 oz) ricotta cheese
1 cup (4 oz) shredded mozzarella cheese, divided
¼ cup grated Parmesan cheese
9 to 10 *Mueller's* lasagne noodles (8 oz), cooked and drained

❶ Prepare sauce mix according to package directions; set aside.
❷ In large skillet heat corn oil over medium-high heat. Add the onion and garlic; stirring quickly and frequently, cook 3 minutes. Stir in spinach, basil, salt and oregano; remove from heat.
❸ In large bowl combine spinach mixture, ricotta, ½ cup mozzarella and Parmesan.
❹ Spread 2 tablespoons prepared sauce in 11x7x1½-inch baking dish; top with ⅓ of the lasagne noodles and ½ the spinach mixture. Repeat sauce, noodles and spinach layers once. Top with remaining lasagne noodles, sauce and ½ cup mozzarella.
❺ Bake in 350°F oven 30 minutes or until bubbly around edge. Let stand 10 minutes before serving. If desired, garnish with sprigs of *fresh basil*.

No-Boil Creamy Spinach Lasagne

It seems that preparing lasagne would be quick and easy if you didn't have to cook the noodles. Great news—you don't! Here's how it's done.

❶ Do not cook lasagne noodles in Creamy Spinach Lasagne recipe, above.
❷ In step 1, prepare sauce mix according to package directions, increasing milk to 1½ cups and water to 1 cup. Prepare ingredients as in steps 2 and 3, above.
❸ In step 4, spread ½ cup prepared sauce in baking dish. Top with ⅓ of the uncooked lasagne noodles and ½ the spinach mixture. Repeat sauce, lasagne noodles and spinach layers once. Top with remaining noodles, sauce and ½ cup mozzarella.
❹ Cover and bake in 350°F oven 30 minutes. Uncover and bake 15 minutes. Let stand 15 minutes before serving.

CREAMY SPINACH LASAGNE,
PESTO TOMATO SALAD (RECIPE, PAGE 35)

Pasta and Cheese Florentine

MAKES
4 SERVINGS

PREP TIME:
15 MINUTES

BAKE TIME:
25 MINUTES

Spinach with cheese sauce—a standard combination in the city of Florence—gives this macaroni dish an Italian flair.

1½ cups milk	8 ounces *Mueller's* elbow macaroni
¾ cup water	(about 1¾ cups), undercooked
1 package (1.8 oz) KNORR Cream of	slightly and drained
Spinach Soup and Recipe Mix	*Mazola No Stick* corn oil
2 cups (8 oz) shredded sharp cheddar	cooking spray
cheese	¼ cup *Devonsheer* or *Old London*
½ teaspoon prepared mustard	plain bread crumbs

❶ In 2-quart saucepan combine milk, water and soup mix. Stirring constantly, bring to boil over medium-high heat; reduce heat and simmer 3 minutes. Remove from heat.
❷ Stir in cheese and mustard until smooth. Stir in macaroni. Spoon into 2-quart casserole sprayed with cooking spray. Sprinkle with bread crumbs.
❸ Bake, uncovered, in 375°F oven 25 minutes or until crumbs are lightly browned.

Pasta Amatriciana

MAKES
4 SERVINGS

TOTAL
PREP TIME:
16 MINUTES

Bacon and caramelized onions give this spaghetti dish its richness. Add a pinch or two of crushed red pepper for character.

8 slices bacon, chopped (about 6 oz)	1 package (1.3 oz) KNORR Parma Rosa
1 large onion, sliced	Pasta Sauce Mix
1¼ cups water	⅛ to ¼ teaspoon crushed red pepper
¼ cup milk	8 ounces *Mueller's* spaghetti, cooked
	and drained

❶ In large skillet cook bacon over medium-high heat, stirring frequently until browned. Drain bacon on paper towels. Pour off all but 3 tablespoons drippings. Set bacon aside. Add onion to drippings. Reduce heat to low; stirring frequently, cook 10 minutes or until onions are golden.
❷ Add water, milk, sauce mix and crushed red pepper. Stirring constantly, bring to boil over medium heat; boil 1 minute.
❸ Stir in reserved bacon. Spoon over spaghetti. Toss to coat. Serve immediately.

Eggplant Rollatini

MAKES
4 SERVINGS

Dazzle your guests with these eggplant roll-ups. They're filled with risotto and smothered with a delicate tomato-and-cheese sauce.

PREP TIME:
35 MINUTES

BAKE TIME:
20 MINUTES

1 package (5.7 oz) KNORR Mushroom
   Risotto Rice Mix
¾ cup (3 oz) crumbled feta cheese,
   divided
1 medium eggplant (about 1 lb), cut
   lengthwise into ¼-inch-thick slices
   (about 12 slices)
⅓ cup *Mazola* corn oil

Salt
Pepper
Dried oregano
Tomato Parma Sauce
   (recipe, below)

❶ Prepare risotto mix according to package directions. Stir ¼ cup cheese into prepared risotto; set aside.

❷ Lightly brush both sides of the eggplant slices with corn oil. Arrange slices in single layer in shallow baking pans. Sprinkle with salt, pepper and oregano. Bake in 400°F oven 10 minutes or until lightly browned.

❸ Meanwhile, prepare Tomato Parma Sauce.

❹ Spoon ¼ cup risotto mixture on wide end of each eggplant slice. Roll up and place seam-side down in 13x9x2-inch baking dish. Spoon Tomato Parma Sauce over eggplant; sprinkle with remaining ½ cup feta cheese.

❺ Bake in 350°F oven 20 minutes or until heated through.

Tomato Parma Sauce

In small saucepan whisk or stir 1¼ cups *milk* and 1 package (1.3 oz) *KNORR Parma Rosa Pasta Sauce Mix* until blended. Add 1 medium *tomato*, coarsely chopped, and 1 tablespoon *butter* or *margarine*. Stirring constantly, bring to boil over medium-high heat. Reduce heat; stirring occasionally, simmer 4 minutes.

Quick & Easy Shrimp Alfredo

Stir ½ pound cooked *shrimp* into the prepared *KNORR Alfredo Pasta Sauce;* toss with 8 ounces *pasta*, cooked.

Mexicali Pasta Bake

MAKES
8 SERVINGS

PREP TIME:
15 MINUTES

BAKE TIME:
15 MINUTES

KNORR White Sauce Mix holds this home-style casserole together. Spiked with cumin and green chilies, it's comfort food with a twist.

2¼ cups milk
1 package (1.8 oz) KNORR White Sauce Mix
½ teaspoon ground cumin
1 tablespoon butter or margarine
2 cups (8 oz) shredded Monterey Jack cheese

1 can (11 oz) corn, drained
1 can (4 oz) diced green chilies, drained
12 ounces *Mueller's* twists or *Twist Trio* (4½ to 5 cups), cooked and drained
½ cup crushed corn or flour tortilla chips

❶ In 2-quart saucepan combine milk, sauce mix and cumin; add butter. Stirring constantly, bring to boil over medium heat; boil 1 minute. Remove from heat.
❷ Add cheese, corn and chilies; stir until cheese melts. Pour over pasta; toss to coat. Spoon into shallow 2-quart baking dish; sprinkle with tortilla chips.
❸ Bake in 350°F oven 15 minutes or until hot and bubbly. If desired, garnish with sliced *red pepper*.

Pasta Genoa

MAKES
4 SERVINGS

TOTAL
PREP TIME:
15 MINUTES

Pesto is a simple sauce made with basil, pignoli (pine nuts), cheese and olive oil. The sauce originated in Genoa, Italy, where fresh basil is frequently used in cooking.

2 tablespoons olive oil
1 large onion, coarsely chopped
1 medium red pepper, cut into thin strips
1 package (10 oz) frozen chopped spinach, thawed and drained
1 medium tomato, coarsely chopped
1 cup milk

1 package (1.2 oz) KNORR Creamy Pesto Pasta Sauce Mix
¼ cup grated Parmesan cheese (optional)
8 ounces *Mueller's* thin spaghetti, cooked and drained

❶ In large skillet heat oil over medium-high heat. Add onion and red pepper; stirring frequently, cook 2 minutes.
❷ Stir in spinach, tomato, milk and sauce mix. Stirring constantly, bring to boil. Reduce heat; stirring constantly, simmer 1 minute. If desired, stir in Parmesan cheese.
❸ Spoon the sauce over the spaghetti; toss to coat. If desired, serve with additional *Parmesan cheese.*

Mexicali Pasta Bake

Pizza Rosa

MAKES
4 SERVINGS

PREP TIME:
10 MINUTES

BAKE TIME:
20 MINUTES

This pizza goes a step beyond the everyday version with its Parma Rosa sauce—rich with Parmesan cheese and seasoned to perfection!

1 package (1.3 oz) KNORR Parma Rosa
   Pasta Sauce Mix
½ cup milk
1 medium tomato, seeded and
   coarsely chopped
1 prepared prebaked pizza crust
   (10-inch diameter)*
1 medium onion, thinly sliced

Toppings: broccoli florets; sliced red,
   yellow or green peppers; sliced
   pepperoni or mushrooms
1 cup (4 oz) shredded mozzarella
   cheese

❶ In small saucepan combine sauce mix and milk; stirring constantly, bring to boil over medium-high heat. Add tomato. Reduce heat; simmer 4 minutes.

❷ Place pizza crust on cookie sheet. Spread with sauce.

❸ Sprinkle with onion, choice of toppings and mozzarella cheese.

❹ Bake in 350°F oven 20 minutes or until cheese melts and crust is heated through.

*For individual pizzas, in step 2, use *Thomas' English muffins* instead of the prebaked pizza crust. Toast split muffins lightly, then top and bake as directed above.

Pizza Variety

Try an easy, new pizza every day. Prepare Pizza Rosa as above but in step 3, top with any of the combinations below.

• Grilled chicken, sliced jalapeño peppers and shredded Monterey Jack cheese.
• Sliced roasted red peppers and crumbled goat cheese.
• Sliced pitted ripe olives, quartered artichoke hearts and shredded smoked mozzarella cheese.
• Cooked shrimp, diced red onion and crumbled feta cheese.
• Sliced tomatoes, crumbled cooked bacon and shredded mozzarella cheese.
• Sliced cooked eggplant and shredded mozzarella cheese.
• Arugula leaves and shredded smoked mozzarella cheese.

PIZZA ROSA

Poultry, Seafood & Meat

These fast & flavorful main dishes are perfect for anytime—and anyone. From down-home comfort food to elegant and exotic fare, the recipes in this chapter are sure to please your family and friends alike.

SANTA FE KABOBS (RECIPE, PAGE 52)

Santa Fe Kabobs

MAKES
4 SERVINGS

PREP TIME:
10 MINUTES

MARINATE
TIME:
30 MINUTES

GRILL OR
BROIL TIME:
10 MINUTES

If you use bamboo or wooden skewers, soak them in water 20 to 30 minutes before threading kabobs (photo, pages 50-51).

1 package (0.8 oz) KNORR Onion Chive Dip Mix
1 cup orange juice
2 tablespoons *Mazola* corn oil
1 tablespoon honey
½ teaspoon ground cumin

1 pound boneless, skinless chicken breasts or thighs, cut into 2-inch pieces
6 small mushrooms
2 red peppers, cut into 2-inch cubes
3 small onions, quartered
   Hot cooked rice (optional)

❶ In medium bowl combine dip mix, orange juice, corn oil, honey and cumin. Add chicken, mushrooms, red peppers and onions; stir gently to coat. Cover; let stand at room temperature no longer than 30 minutes or in refrigerator 1 to 2 hours.
❷ Alternately thread the chicken, mushrooms, red peppers and onions on skewers. Reserve marinade.
❸ Grill or broil kabobs 6 inches from source of heat 10 minutes or until chicken is thoroughly cooked. Turn skewers occasionally, and brush with marinade during first 5 minutes of cooking. If desired, serve on a bed of rice.

Chicken Jambalaya

MAKES
4 SERVINGS

PREP TIME:
15 MINUTES

COOK TIME:
20 MINUTES

The seasonings are in the rice mix, but you might want to add a dash of hot pepper sauce for an extra kick.

2 tablespoons *Mazola* corn oil
¾ pound boneless, skinless chicken (preferably thighs), cut into cubes
5 ounces cooked ham, cut into matchstick strips (about 1 cup)
1 clove garlic, minced
1 can (14½ to 16 oz) whole tomatoes in juice, undrained

1½ cups water
1 package (5.6 oz) KNORR Vegetable Primavera Risotto Rice Mix
1 can (4 oz) diced mild or medium green chilies, drained
1 green pepper, diced

❶ In large skillet heat corn oil over medium-high heat. Add chicken, ham and garlic; stirring frequently, cook 3 minutes.
❷ Add undrained tomatoes, water, rice mix, chilies and green pepper. Bring to boil, stirring to break up tomatoes. Reduce heat. Cover; simmer 20 minutes or until rice is tender, stirring occasionally.

Roast Chicken Normandy

**MAKES
6 TO 8
SERVINGS**

**PREP TIME:
20 MINUTES**

**ROAST TIME:
2½ TO
3½ HOURS**

Apples grow in abundance in the French province of Normandy and are used in many regional foods like this chicken dish.

3 tablespoons butter or margarine, divided
1 medium tart apple, cored and coarsely chopped
1 medium onion, chopped
1 cup water

½ cup apple juice
1 package (4.2 oz) KNORR Chicken Flavor Pilaf Rice Mix
1 egg
1 5- to 6-pound roasting chicken

❶ In large skillet melt 1 tablespoon butter over medium-high heat. Add apple and onion. Stirring quickly and frequently, cook 2 minutes.
❷ Stir in water and apple juice; bring to boil. Stir in rice mix; return to boil. Reduce heat, cover and simmer 10 minutes; cool.
❸ In small bowl beat egg lightly; stir into rice mixture. Spoon rice lightly into cavity of chicken. Tie legs together. Place chicken, breast-side up, on rack in shallow roasting pan. Brush with melted butter.
❹ Roast in 325°F oven 2½ to 3½ hours (about 25 minutes per pound), brushing occasionally with remaining 2 tablespoons butter.

Orange-Peppercorn Chicken

**MAKES
4 SERVINGS**

**TOTAL
PREP TIME:
20 MINUTES**

This sensational creation is shown on the cover.

3 tablespoons *Mazola* corn oil, divided
1 pound boneless, skinless chicken breasts, thinly sliced
3 cups assorted vegetables such as baby carrots and pearl onions, cut lengthwise in half, and sugar snap peas
1 medium red pepper, cut into 1-inch squares

2 shiitake mushrooms, sliced
2 cloves garlic, minced
½ cup water
⅓ cup orange marmalade
¼ cup orange juice
1 package (1 oz) KNORR Peppercorn Sauce Mix

❶ In large skillet heat 2 tablespoons corn oil over medium-high heat. Add chicken, half at a time, and cook 4 minutes on each side or until browned. Remove chicken; set aside.
❷ Heat remaining 1 tablespoon corn oil in skillet. Add vegetables, red pepper, mushrooms and garlic; stirring frequently, cook 5 minutes or until tender-crisp.
❸ Stir in water, marmalade, orange juice and sauce mix. Stirring constantly, bring to boil. Return the chicken to the skillet. Simmer 2 to 3 minutes, stirring occasionally.

Crispy Onion-Baked Chicken

MAKES
4 SERVINGS

PREP TIME:
10 MINUTES

BAKE TIME:
40 MINUTES

Here's an all-in-one crispy coating mix that you can use for chicken, fish or pork.

1 cup *Devonsheer* or *Old London* plain bread crumbs

1 package (1.4 oz) KNORR French Onion Soup and Recipe Mix

3 to 4 pounds bone-in chicken pieces or 8 boneless, skinless chicken breast halves

½ cup *Hellmann's* or *Best Foods* mayonnaise

❶ In large, plastic food bag combine bread crumbs and soup mix.

❷ Brush chicken on all sides with mayonnaise. Place chicken, one piece at a time, in bag; shake to coat well. Arrange chicken on rack in broiler pan.

❸ Bake in 425°F oven about 40 minutes for chicken pieces, 15 minutes for boneless breasts, or until golden brown and tender.

Crispy Onion-Baked Fish Fillets: In step 2, substitute 2 to 3 pounds *sole* or *flounder fish fillets* for chicken. Bake 10 minutes or until fish flakes with fork.

Crispy Onion-Baked Pork Chops: In step 2, substitute 8 (1-inch thick) center-cut *pork chops* for chicken. Bake 25 minutes or until the meat juices run clear.

Flavorful Gravy in Minutes

Prepare 1 package (1.2 oz) *KNORR Roasted Chicken Gravy Mix* as directed. If desired, stir in one of the following:

- 1 cup sliced canned or cooked fresh *mushrooms*
- 2 tablespoons *cranberry-orange relish*

For a creamy flavored gravy, reduce water to ¾ cup and add ½ cup *milk*. Complete as directed above.

CRISPY ONION-BAKED CHICKEN

Chicken Potpie

MAKES
4 SERVINGS

Follow these three quick steps to create one of America's most popular comfort foods. KNORR gravy mix provides the satisfying flavor of homemade gravy.

PREP TIME:
15 MINUTES

BAKE TIME:
10 TO 15 MINUTES

1 tablespoon butter or margarine
1 small onion, chopped
1 package (10 oz) frozen mixed
    vegetables
2 cups cubed cooked chicken
¾ cup water

½ cup milk
1 package (1.2 oz) KNORR Roasted
    Chicken Gravy Mix
1 package (4.5 oz) refrigerated
    buttermilk biscuits*

❶ In 2-quart saucepan heat butter over medium-high heat. Add onion; stirring frequently, cook 3 minutes.

❷ Add vegetables, chicken, water, milk and gravy mix. Stirring constantly, bring to boil. Spoon into 1½-quart casserole. Cut biscuits in half and arrange on top.

❸ Bake in 450°F oven 10 to 15 minutes or until biscuits are browned.

*If desired, prepare half a recipe of your favorite drop biscuits. In step 2, spoon dough on top of mixture. Bake as directed in step 3.

Chicken Cacciatore

MAKES
4 SERVINGS

Cacciatore is Italian for hunter. The most popular dish prepared in this fashion is chicken cacciatore. Serve it over pasta, rice or polenta.

PREP TIME:
15 MINUTES

COOK TIME:
20 MINUTES

1 tablespoon *Mazola* corn oil
4 to 6 chicken thighs (about 1½ lb)
1 medium green pepper, cut into thin
    strips
1 medium onion, chopped
2 cloves garlic, minced

1½ cups water
1 package (2.4 oz) KNORR Tomato
    with Basil Soup and Recipe Mix
½ teaspoon dried oregano
¼ teaspoon pepper
    Hot cooked pasta, polenta or rice

❶ In large skillet heat corn oil over medium-high heat. Add chicken; cook 5 minutes or until browned, turning once. Remove chicken from skillet. Add green pepper, onion and garlic; stirring frequently, cook 5 minutes. Drain off fat.

❷ Add water, soup mix, oregano and pepper. Stirring constantly, bring to boil. Return chicken to skillet. Reduce heat, cover and simmer 20 minutes or until chicken is tender.

❸ Serve over pasta, polenta or rice.

CHICKEN POTPIE

Arroz con Pollo

MAKES
4 SERVINGS

PREP TIME:
10 MINUTES

COOK TIME:
30 TO 35
MINUTES

This version of the popular Spanish rice-and-chicken dish offers all the flavors of the traditional recipe, but with less effort.

1 tablespoon red wine vinegar
¼ teaspoon oregano
½ teaspoon salt
¼ teaspoon pepper
4 boneless, skinless chicken thighs, halved
1 tablespoon *Mazola* corn oil
1 small onion, chopped
2 cloves garlic, minced

1 cup water
1 can (14½ to 16 oz) whole tomatoes in juice, undrained
1 package (4.7 oz) KNORR Spanish Pilaf Rice Mix
1 cup frozen peas
¼ cup small pitted green olives (optional)

❶ In shallow dish combine vinegar, oregano, salt and pepper. Add chicken, turning to coat; set aside.

❷ In 4-quart Dutch oven heat corn oil over medium-high heat. Add chicken; cook about 5 minutes or until browned, turning once. Remove chicken from skillet. Add onion and garlic to skillet; stirring constantly, cook 2 minutes.

❸ Stir in water and undrained tomatoes; bring to boil while crushing tomatoes with back of spoon. Return chicken to skillet; reduce heat, cover and simmer 10 minutes.

❹ Stir in rice mix. Cover and simmer 15 minutes. Add peas and, if desired, olives. Simmer 5 to 10 minutes or until rice is tender.

The Boost of Liquid Broth

Brush *KNORR Concentrated Beef or Chicken flavor Broth* on meat, poultry or fish before broiling, grilling or roasting for a distinctive flavor and added moistness.

Arroz con Pollo

Chicken and Artichokes in Garlic Sauce

**MAKES
4 SERVINGS**

**TOTAL
PREP TIME:
20 MINUTES**

Tasty and quick to make, this dish offers the winning combination that on-the-go cooks desire.

1 tablespoon *Mazola* corn oil
4 boneless, skinless chicken breast
    halves (about 1 lb)
1 cup sliced mushrooms
1 package (9 oz) frozen artichoke
    hearts, thawed
1 cup milk

½ cup water
1 package (1.6 oz) KNORR Garlic
    Herb Pasta Sauce Mix
    Hot cooked pasta or rice

❶ In large skillet heat corn oil over medium-high heat. Add chicken; cook 5 minutes or until lightly browned, turning once. Remove chicken from skillet. Add mushrooms; stirring constantly, cook 3 minutes.
❷ Add artichokes, milk, water and sauce mix. Stirring constantly, bring to boil. Return chicken to skillet. Reduce heat, cover and simmer 5 minutes or until chicken is tender.
❸ Serve over pasta or rice. If desired, garnish with *fresh rosemary*.

Chicken Tetrazzini

**MAKES
4 TO 6
SERVINGS**

**PREP TIME:
10 MINUTES**

**BAKE TIME:
15 MINUTES**

Named for opera singer Luisa Tetrazzini, this recipe makes use of leftover chicken or turkey. Slightly undercook the pasta so it will be perfectly done when it comes out of the oven.

2 cups water
1 cup milk
1 package (0.9 oz) KNORR Mushroom
    Sauce Mix
1 KNORR Chicken Bouillon Cube

1 teaspoon Worcestershire sauce
8 ounces *Mueller's* spaghetti,
    undercooked slightly and drained
2 cups cubed cooked chicken
¼ cup grated Parmesan cheese

❶ In large skillet combine water, milk, sauce mix, bouillon cube and Worcestershire sauce. Bring to boil over medium-high heat, stirring constantly to dissolve bouillon. Reduce heat; stirring frequently, simmer 2 minutes.
❷ In greased 13x9x2-inch baking dish toss spaghetti with 2 cups mushroom sauce mixture. Stir chicken into remaining sauce; spoon mixture onto center of the spaghetti. Sprinkle with Parmesan cheese.
❸ Cover and bake in 350°F oven 15 minutes or until heated through.

Chicken and Artichokes in Garlic Sauce

Paella

MAKES 4 TO 6 SERVINGS

This hearty Spanish dish is named for the large two-handled pan in which it's traditionally cooked and served. However, a large skillet also can be used. Serve salad and bread to round out this one-dish meal.

PREP TIME: 15 MINUTES

COOK TIME: 18 MINUTES

2 tablespoons *Mazola* corn oil
½ pound boneless, skinless chicken (preferably thighs), cut into 1-inch pieces
¼ pound chorizo or Italian sausage, casing removed, sliced ¼-inch thick
1 medium onion, halved and thinly sliced
½ cup diced red pepper
2 cloves garlic, minced

½ teaspoon paprika
¼ teaspoon dried oregano
1¾ cups water
1 package (5.2 oz) KNORR Risotto Milanese Rice Mix
½ pound medium shrimp, shelled and deveined
½ cup frozen peas

❶ In large skillet heat corn oil over medium-high heat. Add chicken; stirring constantly, cook 3 minutes or until lightly browned. Remove chicken from skillet.

❷ Add sausage, onion, red pepper, garlic, paprika and oregano. Stirring frequently, cook 2 minutes. Add water; bring to boil. Stir in rice mix and return to boil; reduce heat, cover and simmer 15 minutes.

❸ Stir in chicken, shrimp and peas. Cover and simmer 3 to 5 minutes or just until shrimp turn pink.

Shrimp Newburg

MAKES 2 SERVINGS

Newburg refers to a rich sauce made with butter, egg yolks and cream. Our version is equally luscious, but it's much lower in calories!

TOTAL PREP TIME: 5 MINUTES

¼ cup (½ stick) butter or margarine
½ pound medium shrimp, shelled and deveined
¾ cup milk
½ cup water

1 package (1 oz) KNORR Newburg Sauce Mix
1 package (4.3 oz) KNORR Original Recipe Pilaf Rice Mix, prepared as directed (optional)

❶ In large skillet heat butter over medium-high heat. Add shrimp; stirring quickly and frequently, cook 1 minute.

❷ Add milk, water and sauce mix. Stirring constantly, bring to boil. Reduce heat and simmer 1 minute, stirring.

❸ If desired, serve over pilaf rice mix.

PAELLA

Fish Amandine

Topped with Hollandaise and almonds, this fast-to-fix dish is fancy enough for a celebration.

½ cup toasted sliced almonds, divided
¼ cup flour
1 pound sole, flounder or perch fillets
½ cup milk, divided
6 tablespoons butter or margarine, divided

1 package (0.9 oz) KNORR Hollandaise Sauce Mix
¾ cup water
1 to 2 teaspoons lemon juice

❶ Set aside 2 tablespoons toasted almonds. Finely chop remaining almonds. In pie plate combine chopped almonds and flour.

❷ Dip the fish fillets in ¼ cup milk, then coat with almond mixture. In large skillet melt 2 tablespoons butter over medium-high heat. Brown the fish, a few pieces at a time, 2 minutes on each side or just until the fish flakes when tested with a fork. Transfer to platter; keep warm.

❸ In skillet heat remaining 4 tablespoons butter over medium heat. Blend in sauce mix. Remove from heat. Stir in water and remaining ¼ cup milk. Stirring constantly, bring to boil over medium-high heat. Reduce heat; simmer, stirring, 1 minute. Stir in lemon juice.

❹ Pour sauce over fish. Sprinkle with reserved toasted almonds.

Floribbean Fish

"Floribbean" is the term chefs have given to foods from Florida that feature flavors adopted from the Caribbean.

1 tablespoon *Mazola* corn oil
¼ cup chopped onion
¼ cup chopped green pepper
2 tablespoons chopped fresh cilantro or parsley

½ cup dry white wine
1 KNORR Vegetarian Vegetable or Fish Flavor Bouillon Cube
1 pound sole, red snapper or cod fillets
2 medium tomatoes, coarsely chopped

❶ In large skillet heat corn oil over medium-high heat. Add onion, green pepper and cilantro. Stirring occasionally, cook 3 minutes or until tender. Add wine and bouillon cube. Bring to boil, stirring to dissolve bouillon cube.

❷ Add fish and tomatoes. Reduce heat, cover and simmer 3 to 5 minutes or just until fish flakes when tested with fork.

Fish Amandine

Grilled Swordfish Bearnaise

MAKES
4 SERVINGS

PREP TIME:
5 MINUTES

MARINATE
TIME:
30 MINUTES

GRILL OR
BROIL TIME:
8 MINUTES

Fish is at its flavor peak when cooked just until done. For best results, follow this rule of thumb: Grill, broil or poach fish for 10 minutes per inch of thickness.

¼ cup (½ stick) butter or margarine
1 green onion, chopped
1 package (0.9 oz) KNORR Bearnaise
   Sauce Mix
1 cup orange juice, divided

1 pound swordfish steak, cut into
   4 serving pieces
   Orange Bearnaise Sauce or Creamy
   Orange Bearnaise Sauce
   (recipes below)

❶ In small saucepan heat butter over medium-high heat. Add green onion; stirring constantly, cook 1 minute. Stir in sauce mix until blended. Remove from heat. Add ¾ cup orange juice. Stirring constantly, bring to boil over medium-high heat.

❷ Pour ¼ cup sauce mixture into 8-inch square baking dish (reserve remaining sauce mixture in saucepan); stir remaining ¼ cup orange juice into sauce mixture in baking dish. Add swordfish, turning to coat. Cover and marinate 30 minutes, turning once. Discard marinade.

❸ Grill or broil swordfish about 6 inches from source of heat 4 minutes on each side or just until fish flakes when tested with fork. Serve with choice of bearnaise sauces, below.

Orange Bearnaise Sauce: To remaining sauce mixture in saucepan, add ¼ cup *orange juice* and 1 teaspoon *lemon juice;* heat through.

Creamy Orange Bearnaise Sauce: In small bowl blend ½ cup *sour cream* into remaining (cooled) sauce mixture.

Easy Roasted Veggies
Roasted vegetables are easy to make, delicious and different.

In a shallow roasting pan, toss a variety of cut-up *vegetables* with 2 to 4 tablespoons *KNORR Concentrated Beef, Chicken or Vegetable Broth.* Roast in 375°F oven for 10 to 25 minutes or until vegetables are tender.

Grilled Swordfish Bearnaise

Shrimp Gumbo

MAKES
ABOUT
5 SERVINGS

PREP TIME:
15 MINUTES

COOK TIME:
23 MINUTES

"Gumbo" comes from the African word for okra, a podlike vegetable used to thicken soups and stews. This dish is a Creole specialty of New Orleans. Add it to your dinnertime menus for a little pizzazz.

3 slices bacon, chopped	1 package (10 oz) frozen sliced okra*
1 large onion, chopped	1 KNORR Chicken or Fish Flavor
1 large tomato, chopped	Bouillon Cube
2 cloves garlic, minced	1 package (4.7 oz) KNORR Spanish
½ teaspoon dried thyme	Pilaf Rice Mix
¼ teaspoon ground red pepper	½ pound medium shrimp, shelled and
3 cups water	deveined

❶ In 3-quart saucepan cook bacon over medium-high heat, stirring frequently until lightly browned. Drain bacon on paper towels. Pour off all but 1 tablespoon drippings. Set bacon aside.

❷ Add onion, tomato, garlic, thyme and ground red pepper to saucepan; stirring frequently, cook 3 minutes.

❸ Add water, okra* and bouillon cube; bring to boil, stirring to dissolve bouillon. Stir in rice mix. Reduce heat, cover and simmer 20 minutes.

❹ Stir in shrimp. Cover and simmer 3 minutes or just until shrimp turn pink. Stir in reserved bacon.

*Or omit okra and, in step 4, add 1 cup frozen *peas* with shrimp.

More Ways with Gumbo

For a change of pace, prepare Shrimp Gumbo as directed above, but substitute ½ pound cubed *chicken breasts* or firm-textured *fish steaks* for the shrimp.

SHRIMP GUMBO

Creole Fish

Onion, green pepper, garlic and tomato give this fish its Louisiana flavor.

1 tablespoon *Mazola* corn oil
1 medium onion, coarsely chopped
1 medium green pepper, coarsely chopped
2 large cloves garlic, minced
1¼ cups water
1 package (2.4 oz) KNORR Tomato with Basil Soup and Recipe Mix

⅛ teaspoon hot pepper sauce, or to taste
1 pound halibut or cod fillets, cut into 4 serving pieces, or 1 pound shrimp, shelled and deveined
Hot cooked rice (optional)

❶ In large skillet heat corn oil over medium-high heat. Add onion, green pepper and garlic. Stirring frequently, cook 5 minutes.

❷ Add water, soup mix and hot pepper sauce. Stirring constantly, bring to boil.

❸ Add fish; reduce heat, cover and simmer 4 minutes or just until fish flakes when tested with fork. If desired, serve with rice.

Rice with Extra Flavor

Serve Creole Fish with rice, but try our flavorful twist. When cooking the rice, omit the salt; add 1 *KNORR Chicken Bouillon Cube* or 2 teaspoons *KNORR Concentrated Chicken flavor Broth* with each 2 cups water; cook as the package directs.

Creole Fish

Shrimp Vera Cruz

**MAKES
4 TO 6
SERVINGS**

**PREP TIME:
20 MINUTES**

**BAKE TIME:
5 MINUTES**

Be careful not to overcook the shrimp. When cooked too long, they lose their delicate flavor and tenderness.

2   quarts (8 cups) water
2   KNORR Chicken Bouillon Cubes, divided
8   ounces *Mueller's* angel hair pasta
2   tablespoons butter or margarine
1   can (15 oz) tomato sauce
1   cup water
¼   cup minced onion
1   clove garlic, minced

½   pound medium shrimp, shelled and deveined
2   tablespoons chopped fresh cilantro
    Mazola No Stick corn oil cooking spray
½   cup sour cream
¼   cup milk
¾   cup (3 oz) shredded Monterey Jack cheese

❶ In 4-quart saucepot bring water and 1 bouillon cube to boil over medium-high heat. Add angel hair pasta; cook 3 minutes. Drain; set aside.

❷ Meanwhile, in large skillet heat the butter over medium-high heat. Add tomato sauce, water, onion, garlic and remaining bouillon cube. Bring to boil, stirring to dissolve the bouillon cube. Stir in the shrimp. Reduce heat and simmer 2 minutes or until the shrimp turn pink.

❸ In saucepot toss pasta, shrimp mixture and cilantro until pasta is coated. Spoon into 11x7x1½-inch baking dish sprayed with cooking spray.

❹ In small bowl combine sour cream, milk and cheese; spoon over pasta. Bake in 350°F oven 5 minutes or until cheese melts.

Bouillon Substitution
Use 2 teaspoons KNORR Concentrated Broth for each bouillon cube.

Grilled Salmon Caliente

MAKES
4 SERVINGS

Grilled or broiled, these salmon steaks are succulent. And as a two-for-one flavor bonus, the KNORR Chili Caliente Dip Mix seasons both the marinade and the creamy salsa.

PREP TIME:
5 MINUTES

MARINATE TIME:
15 MINUTES

GRILL OR BROIL TIME:
10 MINUTES

1 package (1 oz) KNORR Chili
    Caliente Dip Mix, divided
2 tablespoons water
1 tablespoon *Mazola* corn oil
4 1-inch-thick salmon steaks
    (about 1½ lb)

1 cup *Hellmann's* or *Best Foods*
    mayonnaise
1 medium tomato, chopped

❶ In small bowl combine 1 tablespoon dip mix, water and corn oil. Brush on salmon steaks. Cover; marinate at room temperature no longer than 15 minutes or refrigerate up to 2 hours.

❷ For salsa: In small bowl stir remaining dip mix, mayonnaise and tomato until blended. Cover and chill.

❸ Grill or broil salmon 6 inches from source of heat 5 minutes on each side or until fish flakes when tested with fork. Serve with salsa.

Herb Salmon with Fettuccine

MAKES
4 SERVINGS

Exquisite yet light, this supper entrée plays off the natural affinity between seafood and lemon. Add a crisp salad and you'll have a complete meal in minutes.

TOTAL PREP TIME:
10 MINUTES

½ pound salmon fillet
  Salt
  Pepper
2 tablespoons *Mazola* corn oil
1 medium tomato, chopped
    (about 1 cup)
¾ cup water

½ cup milk
1 cup frozen peas
1 package (1.8 oz.) KNORR Lemon
    Herb Sauce Mix
8 ounces *Mueller's* fettuccine, cooked
    and drained

❶ Sprinkle salmon lightly with salt and pepper. In large skillet heat corn oil over medium-high heat. Add salmon; brown about 3 minutes on each side or just until fish flakes when tested with fork. Remove from skillet.

❷ Add tomato to skillet; stirring constantly, cook 1 minute. Blend in water, milk, peas and sauce mix; stirring constantly, bring to boil. Reduce heat and simmer 1 minute.

❸ Stir in salmon, flaking it into large pieces. Spoon sauce over pasta. Toss to coat.

Brandied Beef Filet

MAKES
4 SERVINGS

Demi-glace sauce is rich and brown with an intense flavor. With a touch of brandy, the sauce turns any steak into a sophisticated dish.

TOTAL
PREP TIME:
18 MINUTES

4 1-inch-thick beef tenderloin (filet mignon) steaks (about 1 lb)
1 tablespoon *Mazola* corn oil
1 teaspoon cracked black pepper
2 tablespoons butter or margarine

¾ cup water
¼ cup milk
2 tablespoons brandy or cognac
1 package (1.2 oz) KNORR Demi-Glace Sauce Mix

❶ Brush steaks with corn oil. Sprinkle both sides of steaks with cracked pepper; press pepper into meat.
❷ Heat large skillet over medium-high heat; it should be hot enough to make meat sizzle when it touches pan. Add steaks; brown about 4 minutes on each side or until desired doneness. Remove meat; keep warm.
❸ Reduce heat to medium. Heat butter in skillet until melted. Add water, milk, brandy and sauce mix. Stirring constantly, bring to boil; reduce heat and simmer 1 minute. Serve sauce over steaks.

Oven Pot Roast

MAKES
8 SERVINGS

Serve with mashed potatoes and carrots for a hearty, wholesome dinner.

PREP TIME:
5 MINUTES

⅔ cup vegetable or tomato juice
1 package (0.9 oz) KNORR Spring Vegetable Soup and Recipe Mix

1 (2½ lb) boneless beef chuck roast

ROAST TIME:
2½ HOURS

❶ In small bowl stir vegetable juice and soup mix until blended; set aside.
❷ Place roast on 18x12-inch piece of heavy-duty aluminum foil and place in shallow baking pan. Pour soup mixture over meat. Fold ends of foil over roast and crimp to seal.
❸ Roast in 350°F oven for 2½ hours or until meat is tender.
❹ Transfer meat to serving platter and pour juices over roast.

Brandied Beef Filet

Beef Stew

MAKES
4 TO 6
SERVINGS

PREP TIME:
10 MINUTES

COOK TIME:
1 HOUR,
20 MINUTES

Nothing is quite as satisfying as homemade stew. KNORR French Onion Soup and Recipe Mix saves time and gives this stew its simmered-all-day flavor.

1 tablespoon *Mazola* corn oil	1 package (1.4 oz) KNORR French
1½ pounds boneless beef chuck or	Onion Soup and Recipe Mix
round, cut into 1½-inch cubes	1 teaspoon dried thyme
1 can (14½ to 16 oz) whole tomatoes	1 teaspoon Worcestershire sauce
in juice, undrained	¼ teaspoon pepper
1 cup water	1 pound small red potatoes, quartered
	1 pound baby carrots

❶ In 5-quart Dutch oven heat corn oil over medium-high heat. Add beef, half at a time; cook about 4 minutes or until browned. Remove meat.

❷ In Dutch oven stir undrained tomatoes, water, soup mix, thyme, Worcestershire sauce and pepper. Stirring to crush tomatoes, bring to boil. Return beef to Dutch oven. Reduce heat, cover and simmer 1 hour, stirring occasionally.

❸ Add potatoes and carrots; simmer 20 minutes or until vegetables are tender. If desired, garnish with *fresh thyme sprigs*.

Flavorful Meat Loaf

MAKES
4 TO 6
SERVINGS

PREP TIME:
10 MINUTES

BAKE TIME:
1 HOUR

Turkey is today's lower-cholesterol protein source. Combined with vegetable soup mix, it makes a terrific meat loaf.

1½ pounds ground turkey or lean	½ cup milk
ground beef	1 egg
1 package (1.4 oz) KNORR Vegetable	Tomato sauce (optional)
Soup and Recipe Mix	
½ cup *Devonsheer* or *Old London*	
seasoned bread crumbs	

❶ In medium bowl combine ground turkey, soup mix, bread crumbs, milk and egg.

❷ In foil-lined baking pan shape meat mixture into 8x4-inch loaf.

❸ Bake in 350°F oven 1 hour. Let stand 10 minutes before slicing. If desired, serve with heated tomato sauce.

Beef Stew

Cincinnati Quick Chili

**MAKES
4 SERVINGS**

**PREP TIME:
10 MINUTES**

**COOK TIME:
10 MINUTES**

A Cincinnati chili parlor owner popularized the tradition of serving chili over spaghetti, garnishing it with chopped onion and shredded cheese.

1½ pounds lean ground beef
1 to 2 tablespoons chili powder
1 package (1.4 oz) KNORR French
   Onion Soup and Recipe Mix
1 can (16 oz) red kidney beans, rinsed
   and drained
1 can (14½ to 16 oz) whole tomatoes
   in juice, undrained

½ cup water
   Hot cooked *Mueller's* spaghetti
   (optional)
   Shredded cheddar cheese
   Chopped onions

❶ Heat large skillet over medium-high heat. Add crumbled beef. Stirring frequently, cook about 5 minutes or until lightly browned. Drain off fat. Add chili powder; stirring constantly, cook 1 minute.
❷ Add soup mix, beans, undrained tomatoes and water. Stirring to crush tomatoes, bring to boil. Reduce heat; simmer 10 minutes.
❸ If desired, serve over spaghetti; top servings with cheddar cheese and onions.

Fast and Flavorful Burgers

**MAKES
6 TO 8
SERVINGS**

**PREP TIME:
5 MINUTES**

**GRILL OR
BROIL TIME:
8 TO 14
MINUTES**

KNORR dip mixes give beef or turkey burgers fabulous flavor.

2 pounds lean ground beef or
   ground turkey
1 package (1.1 oz) KNORR Cracked
   Pepper Ranch Dip Mix

6 to 8 *Thomas'* English muffins or
   hamburger buns, split and toasted

❶ In large bowl combine ground beef and dip mix. Shape into 6 to 8 patties.
❷ Grill or broil about 6 inches from heat until desired doneness, turning once.
❸ Serve on toasted English muffins or buns.

Nacho Burgers: In step 1, use 1 package (1 oz) *KNORR Nacho Cheese Dip Mix;* prepare as above.

Caliente Burgers: In step 1, use 1 package (1 oz) *KNORR Chili Caliente Dip Mix;* prepare as above.

Onion-Chive Burgers: In step 1, use 1 package (0.8 oz) *KNORR Onion Chive Dip Mix;* prepare as above.

Cincinnati Quick Chili

Spicy Beef Mandarin

MAKES
4 SERVINGS

TOTAL
PREP TIME:
20 MINUTES

The soul of the Orient punctuates this exotic 20-minute meal. Serve with KNORR Jasmine Rice Pilaf to balance the spiciness.

4	tablespoons soy sauce, divided
3	tablespoons *Argo* or *Kingsford's* cornstarch, divided
¾	pound beef flank or top round steak, cut into thin diagonal slices (tip, below)
1	cup water
⅓	cup apricot preserves or orange marmalade
1	KNORR Beef Bouillon Cube or 4 teaspoons KNORR Concentrated Beef flavor Broth
½	teaspoon ground ginger
¼	teaspoon crushed red pepper
1	clove garlic, minced
3	tablespoons *Mazola* corn oil
2	cups broccoli florets
1	can (11 oz) mandarin oranges, drained
1	package (5.1 oz) KNORR Lemon Herb with Jasmine Rice Pilaf Rice Mix, prepared as directed

❶ In medium bowl stir 2 tablespoons soy sauce with 1 tablespoon corn starch. Add beef; toss to coat. In small bowl stir remaining 2 tablespoons soy sauce, remaining 2 tablespoons corn starch, water, preserves, bouillon, ginger, crushed red pepper and garlic; set aside.

❷ In large skillet or wok heat corn oil over medium-high heat. Add ⅓ of the beef; cook, stirring quickly and frequently (stir-fry), 2 to 3 minutes or until browned. Remove from skillet. Repeat with remaining beef. Add broccoli; stir-fry 2 minutes.

❸ Return beef to skillet. Stir corn starch mixture; pour into skillet. Stirring constantly, bring mixture to boil; boil 1 minute. Remove from heat. Add mandarin oranges. Serve over pilaf rice mix.

Easy Slicing

Meat is easier to slice when partially frozen. Place meat in freezer for 30 to 45 minutes before thinly slicing it for stir-frying.

Spicy Beef Mandarin

Calypso Pork Roast

MAKES
8 TO 10
SERVINGS

PREP TIME:
15 MINUTES

ROAST TIME:
2½ HOURS

Brown sugar, ginger, cumin and orange juice give this splendid roast its Caribbean accent.

1½ cups boiling water
  1 KNORR Chicken Bouillon Cube or
       2 teaspoons KNORR Concentrated
       Chicken flavor Broth
  1 teaspoon ground ginger
 ½ teaspoon ground cumin
 ½ teaspoon pepper
  2 cloves garlic, minced

  1 (4 to 5 lb) bone-in center loin pork
       roast with backbone loosened
  1 cup brown sugar
 ¾ cup orange juice, divided
  1 tablespoon *Argo* or *Kingsford's*
       corn starch

❶ In small bowl stir boiling water and bouillon cube until dissolved; reserve ¾ cup. To remaining ¾ cup bouillon, add ginger, cumin, pepper and garlic.

❷ Place pork roast in 13x9x2-inch roasting pan. Pour gingered bouillon mixture over pork. Cover with foil.

❸ Roast in 350°F oven 2 hours. Remove foil.

❹ In small bowl combine reserved ¾ cup bouillon, brown sugar and ½ cup orange juice; pour over roast. Roast, uncovered, 30 minutes longer or until temperature on meat thermometer reaches 160°F, spooning pan juices over pork several times.

❺ Calypso Sauce: Pour pan juices from roasting pan into large measuring cup; let stand until fat separates from juices. Discard fat. Add enough remaining orange juice to pan juices to measure 2 cups. Stir in corn starch. Pour into small saucepan. Stirring constantly, bring to boil over medium heat and boil 1 minute. Serve with roast pork.

Any Leftover Roast?

If there is leftover meat from the Calypso Pork Roast, use the meat to make an easy, old-fashioned favorite—potpie. Simply substitute 2 cups cubed pork for the chicken in the recipe for Chicken Potpie on page 56.

CALYPSO PORK ROAST

Sausage and Peppers

MAKES
4 SERVINGS

TOTAL
PREP TIME:
20 MINUTES

KNORR Tomato with Basil Soup and Recipe Mix adds zest to this dish.

1 pound sweet or hot Italian sausage
    links, cut into 2-inch pieces
1 medium green pepper, sliced
1 medium onion, sliced
2 cloves garlic, minced
1 package (2.4 oz) KNORR Tomato
    with Basil Soup and Recipe Mix

1¼ cups water
4 Italian bread rolls or 1 package
    (5.2 oz) KNORR Risotto Milanese
    Rice Mix, prepared as directed

❶ In large skillet over medium-high heat cook sausage 2 minutes or until well browned. Pour off all but 1 tablespoon drippings. Add green pepper, onion and garlic; stirring constantly, cook 2 minutes.
❷ In small bowl combine soup mix and water; pour into skillet. Stirring constantly, bring to boil. Reduce heat to low. Partially cover and simmer 10 minutes.
❸ Spoon into Italian rolls or serve with risotto rice mix.

Sausage and Peppers over Pasta: In step 2, increase water to 1½ cups. Serve mixture over hot cooked *Mueller's* pasta.

Pork Chops with Apple-Onion Sauce

MAKES
4 SERVINGS

PREP TIME:
12 MINUTES

COOK TIME:
10 MINUTES

Gone are the days when pork was cooked to a fare-thee-well. These extra-lean center-cut chops are tender and juicy in minutes.

1 tablespoon *Mazola* corn oil
4 center-cut loin pork chops, cut ¾-inch
    thick (about 1½ lb)
1½ cups water
1 medium Red Delicious apple, cored
    and sliced

1 package (1.4 oz) KNORR French
    Onion Soup and Recipe Mix
1 teaspoon cider vinegar

❶ In large skillet heat corn oil over medium-high heat. Add pork chops; cook 6 to 7 minutes or until browned, turning once. Remove pork chops from skillet.
❷ Add water, apple, soup mix and vinegar to skillet. Stirring constantly, bring to boil.
❸ Add pork chops. Cover and simmer 10 minutes.

SAUSAGE AND PEPPERS

Pork with Onion-Herb Risotto

**MAKES
4 SERVINGS**

**PREP TIME:
15 MINUTES**

**COOK TIME:
15 MINUTES**

Risotto is an Italian specialty that normally requires almost 20 minutes of constant stirring to achieve its unique, creamy texture. Now, with the help of KNORR Italian Rice Mix, you can have risotto, fast.

4 bone-in, center-cut rib or loin pork chops, cut ³⁄₄-inch thick (about 1½ lb) Salt Pepper	1 tablespoon *Mazola* corn oil 2 cups water 1 package (6.1 oz) KNORR Onion Herb Risotto Rice Mix

❶ Sprinkle pork chops lightly with salt and pepper. In large skillet heat corn oil over medium-high heat. Add pork chops; cook about 6 minutes or until lightly browned, turning once. Remove pork chops from skillet.
❷ Add water and rice mix; stirring occasionally, bring to boil. Reduce heat to low.
❸ Arrange pork chops over rice mixture. Cover and simmer 15 minutes. Remove from heat; let stand 5 minutes.

Pork Cutlets with Brandy-Mushroom Sauce

**MAKES
4 SERVINGS**

**TOTAL
PREP TIME:
20 MINUTES**

This stylish entrée and KNORR Broccoli au Gratin Risotto Rice Mix pair up for a simply splendid meal.

4 to 6 boneless pork chops, cut ¼-inch thick (about 1 lb) ¼ teaspoon crushed rosemary Pepper 1 tablespoon *Mazola* corn oil 2 tablespoons brandy	1¼ cups milk 1 package (0.9 oz) KNORR Mushroom Sauce Mix 1 package (5.2 oz) KNORR Broccoli au Gratin Risotto Rice Mix, prepared as directed

❶ Sprinkle pork chops with rosemary and pepper. In large skillet heat corn oil over medium-high heat. Add pork chops; cook about 6 minutes or until lightly browned, turning once. Remove pork chops from skillet.
❷ Add brandy to skillet; cook, stirring to loosen browned bits. Add milk and sauce mix. Stirring constantly, bring mixture to boil. Return pork to the skillet. Reduce heat, cover and simmer 3 minutes.
❸ Serve with risotto rice mix.

Pork Oriental

MAKES
4 SERVINGS

TOTAL PREP TIME:
20 MINUTES

The "bite" of peppercorns mingles sublimely with the fruity sweetness of pineapple to give this dish its special character.

2 tablespoons *Mazola* corn oil, divided
¾ pound boneless pork, cubed
1 large onion, cut into wedges
1 large green pepper, cut into 1-inch squares
¾ cup water
⅓ cup apricot preserves

1 package (1 oz) KNORR Peppercorn Sauce Mix
1 can (8 oz) pineapple chunks, drained
1 cup halved cherry tomatoes
Hot cooked rice (optional)

❶ In large skillet heat 1 tablespoon corn oil over medium-high heat. Add pork; stirring frequently, cook 2 minutes. Remove pork.
❷ Heat remaining 1 tablespoon corn oil in skillet. Stirring frequently, cook onion and green pepper 5 minutes or until vegetables are tender-crisp.
❸ Stir in water, apricot preserves and sauce mix. Add pork. Stirring constantly, bring to boil. Stir in pineapple and tomatoes.
❹ If desired, serve over rice.

Fried Rice

MAKES
4 SERVINGS

TOTAL PREP TIME:
28 MINUTES

A little meat goes a long way in this tempting main dish.

½ pound diced uncooked pork
2 tablespoons soy sauce
1 clove garlic, minced
¼ teaspoon ground ginger
2 tablespoons *Mazola* corn oil, divided
¼ cup diced red pepper
1 cup uncooked long grain rice

2 cups water
1 package (1.3 oz) KNORR Hot and Sour Soupmix
2 green onions, sliced (optional)
2 tablespoons slivered almonds (optional)

❶ In medium bowl combine pork, soy sauce, garlic and ginger; toss to coat pork. In large skillet heat 1 tablespoon corn oil over medium-high heat. Add pork and red pepper; stirring quickly and frequently, cook 2 minutes. Remove pork from skillet.
❷ Add remaining 1 tablespoon corn oil to skillet. Stirring constantly, cook rice 2 to 3 minutes or until golden brown. Add water and soupmix. Stirring frequently, bring to boil. Reduce heat to low; cover and simmer 15 minutes.
❸ Stir in pork. Cover and simmer 5 minutes or until rice is tender. If desired, top with green onions and almonds.

Make-Ahead Eggs Benedict

MAKES
8 SERVINGS

PREP TIME:
25 MINUTES

CHILL TIME:
OVERNIGHT

BAKE TIME:
20 TO 25
MINUTES

Here's a dish you can prepare ahead for breakfast or a glorious brunch.

4 *Thomas'* English muffins	8 eggs
8 thin slices Canadian-style bacon (about 5 oz)*	1 package (0.9 oz) KNORR Hollandaise Sauce Mix
1 tablespoon lemon juice or vinegar	1 teaspoon lemon juice

❶ Split and toast English muffins. Arrange muffins cut-side up in 13x9-inch baking dish. Top each muffin half with Canadian bacon; set aside.

❷ Half fill a large skillet with *water;* add 1 tablespoon lemon juice. Heat to simmering.

❸ Break 1 egg into a small dish. Carefully slide egg into water. Repeat with 3 more eggs. Simmer about 5 minutes or until egg yolks are just set. Carefully remove eggs with slotted spoon; blot bottom of spoon dry with paper towel, then place each egg on a muffin. Repeat with remaining 4 eggs.

❹ Prepare sauce mix according to package directions. Add 1 teaspoon lemon juice. Spoon Hollandaise sauce over eggs. Cover and refrigerate overnight.

❺ To serve: Uncover and bake in 350°F oven 20 to 25 minutes or until eggs and sauce are heated through. If desired, garnish with *fresh chives* and chopped *tomato.*

*Or, in step 1, substitute ½ pound blanched *asparagus* for the Canadian-style bacon.

Deluxe Eggs Benedict: Prepare Eggs Benedict as above but in step 1, substitute 5 ounces *smoked turkey* for Canadian bacon; top turkey with ½ pound blanched *asparagus spears.* Complete as directed in steps 2 through 5.

Vegetarian Eggs Benedict: Prepare Eggs Benedict as above but in step 1, omit Canadian bacon. Top English muffin halves with 1 jar (7 oz) *roasted red peppers*, drained and patted dry, and ½ pound sliced blanched *broccoli florets.* Complete as directed in steps 2 through 5.

Salmon Eggs Benedict: Prepare Eggs Benedict as above but in step 1, omit Canadian bacon. Top English muffin halves with 5 ounces thinly sliced *smoked salmon* and ½ pound blanched *asparagus spears.* Complete as directed in steps 2 through 5.

Make-Ahead Eggs Benedict

KNORR Sauces Make Meals Special

It's a cinch to stir up a delicious sauce when you keep KNORR mixes on hand.

KNORR Hollandaise Sauce Mix

Roasted Red Pepper Hollandaise
Prepare 1 package *KNORR Hollandaise Sauce Mix* as directed.
In blender, puree sauce with 1 jar (7 oz) drained *roasted red peppers* until smooth.

Southwest Hollandaise
Prepare 1 package *KNORR Hollandaise Sauce Mix* as directed.
Stir in: ½ cup *prepared salsa*.

KNORR Demi-Glace Sauce Mix

Shiitake Mushroom Demi-Glace Sauce
Prepare 1 package *KNORR Demi-Glace Sauce Mix* as directed.
In step 1, stir in 2 ounces sautéed, sliced *shiitake mushrooms*.

Wine Demi-Glace Sauce
Prepare 1 package *KNORR Demi-Glace Sauce Mix* as directed.
In step 1, stir in 1 tablespoon *red wine*.

KNORR Bearnaise Sauce Mix

Dijon Bearnaise Sauce
Prepare 1 package *KNORR Bearnaise Sauce Mix* as directed.
In step 2, stir in 2 tablespoons *dry white wine*, 1 tablespoon
Dijon-style mustard and ¼ teaspoon *cracked black pepper*.

KNORR Peppercorn Sauce Mix

Bourbon Peppercorn Sauce
Prepare 1 package *KNORR Peppercorn Sauce Mix* as directed.
Stir in: 1 tablespoon *bourbon*.

Creamy Peppercorn Sauce
Prepare 1 package *KNORR Peppercorn Sauce Mix* as directed, but reduce water to 1 cup.
Add: ¼ cup *milk*.

KNORR White Sauce Mix

Cheese Sauce with Macaroni
Prepare 1 package *KNORR White Sauce Mix* as directed, but reduce milk to 2 cups.
Remove from heat.
Stir in: 1½ cups (6 oz) shredded *Swiss* or *cheddar cheese* until melted. Toss with 8 ounces
macaroni, cooked and 1 teaspoon *pepper*.

Creamed Peas and Onions
Prepare 1 package *KNORR White Sauce Mix* as directed.
Stir in: 1 package (10 oz) frozen *peas and pearl onions*, thawed. Stir over low heat until heated through.

KNORR Hunter Mushroom and Gravy Mix

Mustard-Hunter Mushroom Gravy
Prepare 1 package *KNORR Hunter Mushroom and Gravy Mix* as directed.
Stir in: 1 teaspoon *prepared mustard*.

KNORR Classic Brown Gravy Mix

Creamy Brown Gravy
Prepare 1 package *KNORR Classic Brown Gravy Mix* as directed, but reduce water to ¾ cup.
Add: ¾ cup *milk*.

Red Wine Gravy
Prepare 1 package *KNORR Classic Brown Gravy Mix* as directed.
Stir in: 1 tablespoon *red wine*.

KNORR Classic Brown and Onion Lyonnaise Gravy Mix

Mushroom-Onion Brown Gravy
Prepare 1 package *KNORR Classic Brown and Onion Lyonnaise Gravy Mix* as directed.
Stir in: 1 can (4 oz) sliced *mushrooms*, drained.

KNORR Au Jus Gravy Mix

Hot Roast Beef Sandwich
Prepare 1 package *KNORR Au Jus Gravy Mix* as directed.
Add: sliced *roast beef*; heat through.

KNORR Roasted Chicken Gravy Mix

Orange Chicken Gravy
Prepare 1 package *KNORR Roasted Chicken Gravy Mix* as directed, but reduce water to 1 cup.
Add: ½ cup *orange juice*.

KNORR Roasted Turkey Gravy Mix

Creamy Turkey Gravy
Prepare 1 package *KNORR Roasted Turkey Gravy Mix* as directed, but reduce water to ¾ cup.
Add: ½ cup *milk*.

Cranberry Turkey Gravy
Prepare 1 package *KNORR Roasted Turkey Gravy Mix* as directed.
Stir in: 2 tablespoons *cranberry-orange relish*.

Need fresh ideas for what to serve? Here's mealtime inspiration. Whether your plans are simple or fancy, KNORR products provide the key to success.

Brandied
Beef Filet
*(recipe,
page 74)*

Dinners and Parties

Company's Coming

Savory Cheesecake *(recipe, page 12)*
KNORR Onion Chive Dip with *Old London* melba toast
Brandied Beef Filet *(recipe, page 74)*
Roasted potatoes with fresh rosemary
Asparagus with KNORR Hollandaise Sauce
Chocolate mousse cake

Sports Party

Peppery Chicken Nuggets *(recipe, page 10)* with
Peppery Blue Cheese Dip *(recipe, page 9)*
Caliente Avocado Dip *(recipe, page 9)* with tortilla chips
Spinach Dip *(recipe, page 8)* with French bread
or *Old London* melba toast
Cincinnati Quick Chili *(recipe, page 78)*
Ice cream sundaes with assorted toppings

Mediterranean Menu

Hot Artichoke Dip *(recipe, page 8)* with *Old London* melba toast
Quick Gazpacho *(recipe, page 17)*
Paella *(recipe, page 62)*
Wilted Spinach 'n' Pasta Salad *(recipe, page 34)*
Fresh fruit sorbet

Mexican Dinner

Seven-Layer Dip *(recipe, page 16)* with tortilla chips
Baked Nacho Potatoes *(recipe, page 10)*
Black Bean Soup *(recipe, page 16)*
Arroz con Pollo *(recipe, page 58)*
Pineapple wedges

Arroz con Pollo
*(recipe,
page 58)*

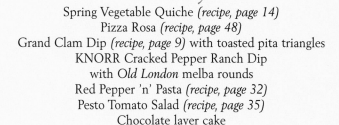

Cocktail Party

Spring Vegetable Quiche *(recipe, page 14)*
Pizza Rosa *(recipe, page 48)*
Grand Clam Dip *(recipe, page 9)* with toasted pita triangles
KNORR Cracked Pepper Ranch Dip
with *Old London* melba rounds
Red Pepper 'n' Pasta *(recipe, page 32)*
Pesto Tomato Salad *(recipe, page 35)*
Chocolate layer cake

Grilled by the Sea

Grilled Swordfish Bearnaise *(recipe, page 66)*
KNORR Onion Risotto Rice Mix
Easy Roasted Veggies *(tip, page 66)*
Mixed greens tossed with balsamic vinaigrette
Strawberries and whipped cream

Grilled
Swordfish
Bearnaise
*(recipe,
page 66)*

Caribbean Cruise

Black Bean Soup *(recipe, page 16)*
Calypso Pork Roast *(recipe, page 82)*
Lemon Vegetables *(recipe, page 25)*
KNORR Original Recipe Pilaf Rice Mix
Pineapple-topped cheesecake

On the Grill

Santa Fe Kabobs *(recipe, page 52)*
KNORR Original Recipe Pilaf Rice Mix
Corn on the cob with Pesto Butter *(tip, page 35)*
Mixed greens tossed with Garden Dill Dressing *(recipe, page 34)*

Santa Fe
Kabobs
*(recipe,
page 52)*

Simply Succulent

Chicken and Artichokes in Garlic Sauce *(recipe, page 60)*
Crusty Italian bread
Lettuce wedge with balsamic vinaigrette
Sliced peaches with raspberries

Seafood Supper

Shrimp Newburg *(recipe, page 62)*
KNORR Original Recipe Pilaf Rice Mix
Steamed broccoli
Apple crisp

Fish Amandine
(recipe,
page 64)

20-Minute Suppers

Streamlined Elegance
Fish Amandine *(recipe, page 64)*
KNORR Risotto Broccoli au Gratin Rice Mix
Sliced tomatoes

Summertime Pasta Dinner
Pasta Genoa *(recipe, page 46)*
Crusty Italian bread
Garden Dill-Cucumber Salad *(recipe, page 34)*

Pacific Coast Dinner
Herb Salmon with Fettuccine *(recipe, page 73)*
Mixed greens with Onion-Chive Dressing *(recipe, page 35)*

Weeknight Entertaining
Brandied Beef Filet *(recipe, page 74)*
KNORR Mushroom Risotto Rice Mix
Green beans

BBQ Burger Bash
Fast and Flavorful Burgers *(recipe, page 78)*
Corn on the cob with Pesto Butter *(tip, page 35)*

Exotically Yours
KNORR Hot and Sour Soup
Spicy Beef Mandarin *(recipe, page 80)*
KNORR Lemon Herb with Jasmine Rice Pilaf Rice Mix
Gingersnaps

Italian Zest
Sausage and Peppers on Italian rolls *(recipe, page 84)*
Mixed greens tossed with Pesto Salad Dressing *(recipe, page 35)*

Tortellini and More
Broccoli Cheese Sauce with Tortellini *(recipe, page 39)*
Sliced tomatoes
Baby carrots

Spicy Beef
Mandarin
*(recipe,
page 80)*